D1268202

BABEL'S TOWER

Printed and bound in Canada

Design Paolo Greco
Typesetting Sam Sumack
Printing Livingstone Printing Limited

ISBN 0-88963-001-1

Thornwood Publications
141 Avenue Road
Toronto, Ontario
M5R 2H7

William Krehm

BABEL'S TOWER

The Dynamics of Economic Breakdown

Thornwood Publications,
141 Avenue Rd.,
Toronto, Ontario M5R 2H7,
Canada

To François Perroux

Contents

Preface

Whoever has challenged an established dogma will have come away with an odd experience. For years the orthodox will ignore a self-evident relationship, and show scant sufferance to those drawing attention to it. And then, when it can no longer be disregarded, some recognition will be given it. But somehow this will constitute an erosion of its full significance. The experts will tend to treat it as something so self-evident as hardly to merit the attention which, indeed, they denied it. Without intermediate staging, the transition from heresy to commonplace is made.

Above all there will be a total lack of curiosity as to why the obvious should have eluded them so long; or what it was that permitted others to predict the bruising collisions with reality that caused the turnabout.

But what difference does that make? A considerable one. Deducing reality from a bump on our forehead is a very different matter from seeing it in advance. And so long as we fail to ask what it was that blinded us to the traumatic fact, we shall be storing up further surprises for ourselves. We shall go on moving like caterpillars with antennas on their rumps instead of their heads.

Some fifteen years ago I began working on the notion that the relative growth of the public sector must feed a structural component of price rise into our economy. At the time a three percent annual price increase was considered something of an emergency in North America. My theory ran counter to the central tenet of established doctrine that identified *any* price rise with an excess of demand. By grace of a self-equilibrating mechanism assumed to exist in our economy, it was believed that such higher prices should tend to choke off demand and bring prices back to their equilibrium level. When this failed to take place, governments tried forcing the economy to conform to the theory. And once more — predictably — the opposite occurred. More often than not, deflationary policy made for still more 'inflation'. Unemployment and climbing prices flourished side by side, giving rise to an alleged 'paradox'.

By 1970 I was finally able to have a paper published on the subject — in France. In 1975 I arranged for the publication of my book *Price In A Mixed Economy — Our Record Of Disaster*. It identified other structural components of price rise, and analyzed their interrelationships and feedbacks. The concept of pluralistic price was developed, reflecting the growing pluralism of our economy. Viewed in such a perspective, not all price increase could be regarded as just plain 'inflation'; for that would be setting up a false aggregate that lumped together factors having distinct causes. Part of our 'inflation' merely reflected the cost of the growing basket of public services that we have been drilled to ignore. And since we have been kept unaware of their full cost, we have been prodigal in demanding more of them.

To complicate matters still more, the neo-Keynesian school saw in taxation a tool for stabilization; it helped keep prices down by 'syphoning off excess demand'.

Since then the business community, the public, our governments, and academic economists – in roughly that sequence – have awakened to the fact that taxation actually contributes to push up prices.[1] And yet there has been little serious effort to explore this relationship in depth. We have had instead a stampede away from yesterday's altars. Rather than accepting *structural* price rise as part of the price tag for public services, increased public services *per se* have come to be regarded as the evil. Health, educational, and other budgets are being slashed as irresponsibly as they were expanded only yesterday. Useful programs in which much investment has already been made have been abandoned. Little distinction is drawn between waste in the public sector and public services that we may really need. And finally there has been little consideration of how we might enlist the private sector to help deliver public services more efficiently.

The one thing that has gone unquestioned in this frantic swing-about is the assumption that stable prices are feasible in our pluralistic economy. We go on taking for granted not only that 'inflation' can be 'licked', but that it must be 'licked' before we can address ourselves to society's other problems. The fact that these 'other' problems concern our physical survival and have time-leads that call for policy initiated decades in advance, does not seem to trouble our 'inflation fighters'. That is why, despite our vocal concerns about our environment, we settle hopes on revived automobile production to pull us out of a recession that is to an extent self-inflicted.

By a quaint combination of rarefied theory and white-caning, economists have locked themselves in a vicious circle. And they make it difficult for others to help them out of it. Whatever new idea is offered is likely to be subjected to an exacting test: 'We are empiricists. Show us what practical policies can be derived from your model.' But the practical tests by which any new theory is to be judged are inevitably dictated by the assumptions of the old doctrine: 'Can the new model cure inflation?'

Never for a moment are we allowed to step outside the preconceptions of the established theory to *question its premises*. Indeed the questions we should ask cannot even be formulated in its idiom: 'To what extent *is* it possible to eliminate rising prices in a pluralistic economy?'; 'How can we distinguish the components of price increase due to excess demand from those resulting from

1 David Warsh and Lawrence Minard, *Inflation Is Now Too Serious a Matter to Leave to the Economists, Forbes,* November 15th, 1976, relate rising prices to rising taxation in a delightful satire. Rather than from the wisdom in the economics journals, the revelation came to the authors from an old Clark Gable movie on late television. Accordingly they propose nominating Gable for the next Nobel Prize in economics.

the structural changes in our economy?'; 'How may we design policies to eliminate the inequities caused by the structural price gradient?'; 'How may we harness the structural price gradient for socially desirable ends?'

This explains why I found it necessary to include a chapter on philosophy in a book on economics. Twice in forty years the profession that is assigned humanity's heavy thinking on economic matters has brought us to the brink of disaster. Basically this has been due to the skittish use that it has made of the resources of the mind.

In Chapter Two, I have turned to the methods of system dynamics to help us avoid the pitfalls of conventional theory. These have the merit of circumventing everybody's dogma: they plot causal circuits as they can be observed, with a special alertness to feedbacks. For introducing me to the literature on the subject I am indebted to Professor Samuel Madras of York University. Professor Madras has contributed an appendix where the method is applied specifically to housing problems.

My earlier book took its departure from a critique of marginalist theory and traced the malcorrespondences with reality that this imposed on economic thought. In this volume my approach is another, but the reasoning rests on considerations and techniques developed in detail in the earlier work. On the other hand concepts such as entropy and tax-bonding that were touched upon there are elaborated more fully in the present book. Much of what I have to say on economic entropy appeared in a paper published in *Cahier d'Economie Appliquée* of Paris, 1977, tome 1.

Thomas Kuhn's *The Structure of Scientific Revolutions*[2] has become the fashionable thing to quote in papers on economic theory. That suggests that many economists sense the need for a drastic rethinking of their fundamental theory. But from there to applying Kuhn's conclusions to their discipline lies a considerable stretch – roughly the distance between owning a surgery textbook and performing an appendectomy on yourself.

Let us hear what Kuhn has to say on the point: 'One of the things a scientific community acquires with a paradigm is a criterion for choosing problems that, while the paradigm is taken for granted, can be assumed to have solutions. . . . Other problems . . . are rejected as metaphysical. . . .' 'A paradigm can, for that matter, even insulate the community from those important problems that are not reducible to the puzzle form, because they cannot be stated in terms of the conceptual and instrumental tools the paradigm supplies'. 'Almost always the men who achieve these fundamental inventions of a new paradigm have been either very young or very new to the field whose paradigm they change'.[3]

So great is the trauma of replacing a paradigm for those working within it, that the operation almost invariably strikes them as a violent assault. And yet this can never be accomplished as a neat, well-mannered, inside job, achieved by further refinement of the familiar model.

The model that we must uproot takes on many shapes and forms. One thing these have in common: the assumption that somewhere at the heart of our economy there is a benign, self-balancing mechanism at work. Once this is

---

2 University of Chicago Press, 1970.

3 pp. 37, 68, and 90.

expressed in mathematical terms – by equating to zero the first derivatives of differential equations to obtain the equilibrium points – the position becomes as impregnable as any feudal donjon with its moat and draw-bridge. I propose to outflank these fortifications. As in my previous book, I will simply avoid the idiom of marginal theory. I will assume no equilibrium points to exist, unless their existence has been proved from the world of reality.

I am aware that this will not be well taken by many mathematical economists. Fortunately I can offer them some consolation. There is a great deal that economists could borrow from mathematics other than the maximisation technique that has up to now made up so much of their bag of tricks.

In his delightful *Concepts of Modern Mathematics*[4] Ian Stewart quotes a certain Matthew Pordage: 'One of the endearing things about mathematicians is the extent to which they will go to avoid any real work'. 'Ploughing straight through is not always the quickest way to make progress. It may be better to go around an obstacle rather than charge headlong into it. It is much the same in mathematics. . . . Often the key to further progress is to stand back, forget about the special problem, and see if you can spot any general features of the surrounding area which might be of use'.

Very often the answer will be provided by the common structure that one situation will have with a completely different one in a quite remote field of mathematics

It is regrettable too, that economists make no use of the labor-saving device *reductio ad absurdum,* that is so dear to mathematicians. Undoubtedly this is due to the fact that they start by putting the absurd into their premises. From there, there is no place to go.

During the decades when they were proving from their equilibrium models that increased taxation was a means of keeping prices stable, there was an elegant, indirect way of proving that this could not possibly be the case. For were that true, all that would be necessary to 'lick inflation' would be to increase taxes and apply the proceeds to subsidize producers to lower their prices. Prices would thus be kept down on a double count. Nonsense? But of course. It is in fact *reductio ad absurdum.* Had they resorted to such lazy methods, economists could have saved themselves much labor and our economies many hundreds of billions of dollars of output.

Indirect reasoning might have also been useful to leftist thinkers in their exceedingly modest efforts to get to the bottom of our price problem.[5] For had they considered the doctrinal disputes in their own camp early in the century, they would have anticipated much of the contents of this book. Over seventy-five years ago Eduard Bernstein created an uproar in the European

---

4 Penguin Books, Baltimore, 1975, pp. 27 and 158.

5 A technical problem of economic theory became snarled in the tactics of an ideological contest. Ideas came to be classified according to whether they helped or hindered *The Reader's Digest's* perennial crusade against public services. For a discussion of the long shadow cast by *The Reader's Digest* on the theoretical thought of our economics faculties see John H. Hotson, *Stagflation and the Bastard Keynesians,* University of Waterloo Press, 1976, pp. 8, 16, 17, 49, 74, and 205.

Socialist movement by questioning the Marxist prognosis of a progressive impoverishment of the masses. In doing so he was greatly influenced by the Fabians whom he had known during his years of exile in Britain.[6]

The growth of the public sector these past forty years has borne out many of Bernstein's predictions. Bernstein and his British mentors, however, had passed lightly over an important point: the doctrine of the gradual evolution towards socialism implied momentous changes in the behavior of price. In their view the public sector could be expected to grow from let us say ten percent of the economy to forty, to fifty, to eighty, even to ninety percent. With this the price structure of the shrivelling private sector would be called upon to support the redistributional function of the public sector. Surely price signals could not then be considered just a reading of the balance between supply and demand. And thus the whole matter of price stability would have to come up for re-examination. The irony of it all is that it was just about this time that many Fabians abandoned the labor theory of value for marginal utility that excluded even the possibility of posing such questions.

Bernstein and the Fabians can be pardoned for not having foreseen the problem. It belonged to the dim future; at the time even the concepts and statistics of national income accounting hardly existed. It is more difficult to excuse their descendants for the same oversight.

Our ability to think in a timely way about our real economic problems is a key part of society's apparatus for survival. Without it we shall be helpless to adapt to the accelerating transformations that our economy is undergoing.

That places a responsibility not only upon those who write, but on those who read books treating of these matters.

---

6. Joseph A. Schumpeter, *History of Economic Analysis,* Oxford University Press, New York, 1954, pp. 532, 763, 880, 883.

Chapter One

ROOTS

Much of our intellectual history of the past fifty years has been a revolt against the quaint standards of the Victorians. From a critique of their politics and their customs we long ago worked our way into their bedrooms and brothels, and ransacked every cranny of their souls. To this there is a single exception: in our economic thinking we are still imprisoned in a Victorian code. It is unfortunate that historians should as a rule have been ignorant and even disdainful of economic theory. Otherwise, William Stanley Jevons and Alfred Marshall, the British founding fathers of marginal theory, would certainly have found places in the portrait gallery of Lytton Strachey and his successors.

Until about a century ago most thinking on economic matters was being done in terms of labor theory of value. It had had the merit of presenting the larger economic issues in the perspective of the social division of labor. Directly or indirectly, the amount of labor that entered into the production of a commodity was seen as the determinant of its value and, in the long run, of its market price. As all theories must, the labor theory left a great deal unexplained; but it enabled economists to correct the astigmatisms of earlier schools. That was so in the case of the Mercantilists who considered the precious metals as 'value' *par excellence,* and the Physiocrats who attributed to agriculture unique, almost mystical properties as the only really productive pursuit. The wisest thing that can be said about the Mercantilists and the Physiocrats was not that their theories were absolutely wrong, but that the aspects of reality singled out by them were no longer the crucial ones in the youthful capitalist economies.[1]

---

1 William Krehm, *Price in a Mixed Economy — Our Record of Disaster,* Thornwood Publications, Toronto, 1975, Chapter 11, develops the theme of the relativistic nature of all value theories.

The trouble with the labor theory of value was quite the opposite: it brought the key relationships of the capitalist economy into too glaring focus. In the hands of David Ricardo it had served the industrialists well in establishing the harmful nature of monopolies and tariff restrictions. The analysis for such demonstrations was done in units of labor: by that theory economic phenomena were given a common denominator, an objective unit.

Relating value to labor, however, was a dangerous procedure in an age when wages were still set by what was needed to keep body and soul together. Long before Karl Marx appeared, social-minded writers were finding in Ricardo's writings proof of labor's exploitation.

This gave rise to a moral malaise of the British middle class. The Victorians were not given to deep ethical introspection; they could not go on living with the Ricardian theory in any degree of comfort. This was particularly the case since for them its great historical purpose had been fulfilled with the repeal of the Corn Laws.

At this point marginal theory made its providential appearance. It shifted the whole discussion of value from the sphere of production, where it had begun to get rough and unmannerly, to the market. Everything – not only price but income distribution – was explained in terms of impersonal market forces. Instead of assessing the workers' input by how long they worked, their contribution was *defined* by what they were paid. Value was simply where supply met demand and the market was cleared. Couched in differential equations, the argument became 'scientific', and beyond questioning. For this was an age when religious fervor was coming to be replaced with the worship of science. In place of classes and a social question, economists were left with traders on a variety of markets.

There remained in fact no other way of reasoning on economic subjects than in terms of supply and demand. The social question, which had lain like a dead rat in the chalice of Victorian piety, was done away with. Marginal theory provided everything that could be wished for – the benediction of providence and a fig-leaf for the shameful parts of society. The prestige of science swept along even professional doubters like G. B. Shaw. It was no small achievement.[2]

But it all rested upon a misunderstanding. The new theory undertook to deduce a conclusion about the real world *from* mathematics instead of *by* mathematics from relevant social data. And the differential

2 George Bernard Shaw, *The Intelligent Woman's Guide to Socialism,* Constable and Company Ltd., London, 1929, p. 466.

equations of marginal theory became a status symbol. Any economist who merely expressed himself in 'literary' non-mathematical form, was adjudged a second-class citizen – no matter what he might have to say.

A little mathematics can be a dangerous acquisition; the antidote, however, is strictly homeopathic – still more mathematics. For if mathematics teaches us anything, it is the endless variety of possible relationships. The founding fathers of marginal theory, Léon Walras and Jevons, had more reverence for mathematics than knowledge in the field. They seized upon the maxima-minima device of elementary calculus and mistook its use for a guarantee of scientific method.[3]

The only input that could be fitted into their model was that with an increase of supply price goes down, and with an increase of demand it goes up. The model purported to show that the market was self-equilibrating and ever tending towards equilibrium points. To make use of maximization, they needed a continuous mathematical function – one that moved smoothly: otherwise the technique would simply not be applicable. To obtain such a function they patched together their definition of a 'pure and perfect market'.

This meant that buyers and sellers were of such insignificant power and dimension that whatever they might do or leave undone individually could not affect the market. Moreover, they went right on buying and selling until the increase of their 'satisfaction' for the last unit bought or sold amounted to zero. In this way their 'satisfaction' was maximized. They had perfect knowledge of the market in one sense – they knew exactly at what price the market would be cleared to give them zero return on their last purchase or sale. And yet, though like *idiots savants* they could calculate instantaneously the price that would maximize their return, in all other respects they had zero foresight, hindsight, and side-sight. They were unable to calculate the average costs of what they were selling – even to try doing that would be to incur the sin of 'full costing'. They were helpless to benefit from their previous experience, or to enquire what their competitors or customers might be up to. Such arbitrary suppositions are deduced from the need of our thinker to maximize *his* satisfaction by being able to solve his differential equations, equating their first derivatives to zero. That is how this fateful model got its equilibrium points.

3 'As the complete theory of almost every other science involves the use of that (differential) calculus, so we cannot have a true theory of economics without its use'. W. Stanley Jevons, *The Theory of Political Economy,* London, Macmillan Limited, 1911, p. 67.

Time and again this ritual of reshaping the world to obtain a manageable set of equations was torn to shreds by distinguished critics, but the practice went right on. And for good enough reasons. Without such assumptions a mountain-range of scholarship and libraries of text-books would become obsolete. At least in this area our world is not steered by principles of built-in obsolescence.[4]

But, of course, we are told that this doctrine is not supposed to have any relevance to the real world, and it is not meant to be normative. It could in fact be put down as simply another of those harmless games *homo ludens* is given to, the sort of thing that Johan Huizinga saw as the source of man's Protean powers.[5] One detail stands in the way of this interpretation: in this instance *homo ludens* combines some of the less engaging traits of card-cheat and snobbish clubman.[6]

There is in fact a note of Victorian hypocrisy about the way in which conventional theory protests that its conclusions are not normative; and then by means of a vocabulary loaded with normative implications, smuggles in policy recommendations drawn from its doctrine.

---

4 In the mechanics of this unrelativistic theory, there are some strange parallels with the relativistic mechanics of Einstein. The adaptation of price to the market is the fastest moving item in this universe, i.e. price is the one source of information. If anything responded faster its laws of causality would break down. It is thus the equivalent of 'c', the velocity of light, in relativistic physics.

In an effort to break out of this box Axel Leijonhuvud hit upon the formulation that the volume of production adapts to market conditions faster than price. In the event of overproduction instead of price dropping instantaneously, the producers simply produce less, thus giving rise to the snow-balling unemployment effect that Keynes studied. (Axel Leijonhuvud, *'On Keynesian Economics and the Economics of Keynes — a Study of Monetary Theory*. Oxford University Press, 1968, p. 53).

Once you accept the speed of price adaptation as the fastest phenomenon in your universe, not a single of the wonders with which Einstein bewildered the layman is missing. Yardsticks change their lengths; clocks slow down — a half-century and more. And in social accounting, government expenditures shrink and even vanish by a formula that evokes Einstein's $\sqrt{1-\frac{v^2}{c^2}}$

5 Johan Huizinga, *Homo Ludens, a study of the play-element in culture,* Boston, Beacon Press, 1972.

6 Those who question the dogma of marginal theory are likely to be treated as as though they were non-existent. That in the English-speaking world has been fate of François Perroux who wrote the definitive critique of marginal theory a generation ago. I deal with the work of this remarkable French school in Krehm, op. cit. Chapter Four.

What went up had to come down, and what went down had to come up – it was as simple as that. This yo-yo interpretation of reality helped get the world into grave trouble in the thirties; it is at the bottom of our difficulties today.

The established theory of the thirties held that the sharp drop of prices during the Depression would in itself trigger a flood of buying and bring about recovery – there were after all so many bargains around! This article of faith, known as 'Say's Law', held that by its very production every commodity tended to create its own market. And when instead unemployment went on snowballing, orthodox economists blamed trade unions and spendthrift government for preventing the self-balancing mechanism in the economy from taking over.

Today our growing unemployment has been substantially initiated by governments to help bring prices into line. And when it fails to do so, the fault is once again placed upon culprits sabotaging the balancing act of providence. Who the guilty might be depends upon individual tastes. For J. K. Galbraith it is Big Labor and Big Business (never Big Government). For Milton Friedman it is Big Government. Bankers are likely to tell you that it is too much money supply. Governments will hold that it is Too Great Expectations (of the other fellow, of course, never of governments). All these explanations take their departure from the dogma that if it were not interfered with, the economy would on its own be returning to price stability. Indeed, it would never have left it.

It took J. M. Keynes several years to work his way out of the straight-jacket in which marginal theory had laced economic thinking. To do so he had to improvise a value theory that permitted him to deal with the problem of effective aggregate demand.[7] By this heroic device he not only helped the world move away form the brink of the precipice; he brought to economists a prestige they had never known before. From sparsely nurtured academics who sang hymns to The Invisible Hand in ivory towers, they were transformed into wizards who could increase the national income by billions. Overnight they came to move easily in

---

7 'I sympathize, threfore, with the pre-classical doctrine that *everything is produced by labour. . . .* It is preferable to regard labour, including, of course, the personal service of the entrepreneur and his assistants, as the sole factor of production, operating in a given environment of technique, natural resources, capital equipment, and effective demand. This partly explains why we have been able to take the unit of labour as the sole physical unit which we require in our economic system, apart from the units of money and time'. *The General Theory of Employment, Interest, and Money*, London, Macmillan Limited, 1936, p. viii.

the councils of the mighty.

Inevitably Keynes became something of a patron saint for most economists. That was a heavy burden to thrust upon any mortal, and because of it much injustice is being done to his memory in our day. It has become impossible to carry on a discussion of inflation without it becoming a session on Keynesology. And when that happens, it is as though we had entered a holy boneyard. Around us the sacred relics lie in heaps; the tibias are mixed with the femurs. Here and there something will turn up that did not belong to the saint at all, but proves to be the jawbone of some later ass.[8]

And yet what should be more readily identifiable than the saint's bones is his spirit. The Bursar of King's was a man of practical genius; he had a gift for bridging the gap between the real world and the constructs of theory. He was impatient with any theory that obstructed the practical task he had in hand. Some academic economists have seen this as a defect, and have been tempted to assign him to the back of their Economics IE class.

However, if we tried imitating Keynes in this respect, we could save ourselves a peck of trouble. We would realize that there is no sense looking too hard in Keynes for answers to the problems of our contemporary world. For in crucial ways the world has changed beyond recognition since his time.

In the thirties the problem that preoccupied Keynes was finding sufficient demand to keep the economy going. He came up with the most whimsical work-making schemes to highlight his point that any economic activity – no matter what its intrinsic merit – would be helpful to start the stalled wheels of industry turning.

This is hardly our problem today. An advanced pluralism has taken over in our society – something that did not remotely exist in the thirties. At that time the state confined itself largely to its traditional administrative function plus a modest outlay on such items as education. Today in some advanced countries public spending has surpassed forty and even fifty percent of the Gross National Product.

---

8 Anyone familiar with Leijonhuvud's book cited will know what I refer to. The Neo-Keynesians have not only attributed to Keynes a belief in the self-equilibrating market, but to make this plausible have converted him into an advocate of high interest rates. And yet if there was one motive that ran through all Keynes's writings, it was the desirability of low interest rates. He took a dim view of both the merits and prospects of the *rentier:* he foresaw his 'euthanasia' through interest approaching and even passing beyond zero.

Such statistics, however, understate the change. In Keynes's day the laws of the market had scarcely been challenged; its ethic – 'you get what you pay for' – was still taken to be a universal truth.[9] Today other ethics exist in symbiosis with that of the market. A growing part of the national income is allotted by redistributional principles – according to social need as determined by political process. The vehicle for this transformation has been the public sector – both by its direct expenditure and by the transfer payments passing through its hands. Technological, demographical developments and the rapid urbanization of our culture have called for costly infrastructures that only the state can provide. This has also imposed standards of education undreamt of in the thirties. As a result a ravening demand for capital has arisen without precedent in the history of the world.

We can hardly fault Keynes for having foreseen rather little of this. He rearranged his basic theory only enough to allow him to get on with the job he had set himself. Essentially his was an *ad hoc* performance with many loose and dangling ends. That troubled a later generation of stylists among his followers. And after his death many of these applied themselves to smoothing out such blemishes. In doing so, they eliminated those infusions of reality that made up the core of Keynes's contribution.

The so-called Neo-Keynesians produced a mathematical model that oscillated about equilibrium points set by the aggregate demand that the policy-makers pumped into the system. Any imbalance on any market invariably released countervailing forces that tended to bring the system back to the equilibrium points to which it had been 'fine-tuned'. Say's Law was rededicated as the keystone of this structure. Walras was wedded to Keynes.

But all this was based upon a comedy of errors. To break out of the vicious circle of marginal theory, Keynes had improvised a labor unit of value; for the problem of adequate demand could not even be formulated in an idiom in which supply and demand by definition tended to balance at all times. He therefore shifted the argument to real terms and excluded the problem of price levels. Improperly understood, this device gave rise to Paul Samuelson's 45° line which marked out the locus of equivalence of aggregate supply and demand. A whole genera-

9 The concept of profit as the 'dominant revenue' of a specific historical period is of key importance in this connection. This idea was developed by François Perroux and others of the French school and simply has no counterpart in the literature of the Anglo-Saxon countries.

tion of economists have been trained to do their reasoning within this framework that simply by-passes the whole subject of price.[10]

Blocked by marginal theory in his attempts to get at his problem, Keynes had resorted to an *ad hoc* means of reckoning – much as you might take off your boots and do your counting on your fingers and toes if your arithmetic has broken down. Under such circumstances that would be a shrewd if primitive thing to do. The point to remember, however, is that if you plan covering any distance after such an exercise, you must put your boots on again. This the Neo-Keynesians forgot to do. Because Keynes had shunted out the whole price problem to deal with aggregate demand, the Neo-Keynesians concluded that price stability would present no difficulty if only you balanced supply and demand. They brought back the whole baggage of a self-equilibrating market.

And that is how we find our thinking on economic matters still paralyzed by the dogma that Keynes had tried expunging in the thirties. Price increases are automatically identified with an excess of demand. It is taken for granted that prices can be brought down by decreasing demand. Actually price in our mixed economy may rise for a variety of causes that have nothing to do with the supply-demand balance. They may merely reflect structural changes in the economy.

A great deal of prejudgment can be built into the language we use. Ethnologists have found the vocabulary of primitive peoples to have developed along functional lines: they reflect the tasks and interests of their cultures. Eskimos will thus have scores of different words for snow to our one. For them the distinctions expressed in these have vital significance.

Ours is a very different economy than it was forty years ago. Because of that it is almost inevitable that the economic terminology of that period should have become dysfunctional today. If we had a single word for table-fork and pitch-fork, we would not find it helpful either for dining or for cleaning out our barns.

The term 'inflation' is an instance of such semantic dysfunction. The word derives from *inflare* – 'to blow up'. Inevitably that sneaks in the inference that the phenomenon is reversible. That may have been all right when we were dealing with the price movements of the trade cycle, and knew from experience that what went up had to come down. That, however, cannot be taken for granted with our price movement

---

10 See John H. Hotson et al., *Stagflation and the Bastard Keynesians*, University of Waterloo Press, 1976, p. 27.

of today.

Our minds in fact have been programmed by the reigning theory to come up with the wrong answers. Let us take the expression 'trade-off' of inflation against unemployment that sounds so realistic and down-to-earth. It assumes a one-to-one relationship between inflation and unemployment. This was the basis of the ill-starred Phillips Curve that claimed to deduce such a correlationship from British statistics over the past century. On the strength of this theory, the economies of much of the Western world were repeatedly subjected to deflationary drubbings by their governments at a cost in human anguish that no statistician will ever establish. All this could have been avoided if we had considered that the relationship that the Phillips Curve purported to deduce was ruled out by the social realities over the period covered. At the beginning of that span trade unions were practically non-existent, social insurance unheard of, and government played a quite different role than it does today. If economists were to develop some sensitivity for such factors, they could spare themselves many false starts.

The fact is that such concepts as prices, wages, and even unemployment have meaning only in relation to a given *social and economic field*. The price of a commodity will reflect not only the specific costs of its own production, but the context of relationships around it. The growth of the public sector within the economy will result in a growing layer of taxation in its price to pay for public services; anti-discrimination legislation may have altered its labor costs, and so forth. To help organize our thinking on such matters we must look to field theory in physics.[11]

Conventional economic theory has ignored the institutional field

11 It is impossible to describe an electro-magnetic field adequately by a one-to-one treatment of the electrical charges in it — the equivalence of the 'trade-off' concept in economics. Firstly, to describe the field you must take into consideration the influence of charges at every point in space. And since the number of such points is infinity to the third degree, your degrees of freedom for the field are similarly infinite. Your 'trade-off' would then have to be not between two isolated charges but between one charge and those that may exist at any of these infinite points of space. Secondly, the interaction of a charge and the field would be the sum of different kinds of influences involving quite different variables associated with the charge (e.g. its mass, its electrostatic quantity, its velocity) and different components of the field (its electrical intensity, its magneic induction) according to quite distinct mathematical laws. See, for example,: D. E. Rutherford, *Vector Methods applied to differential geometry, mechanics, and potential theory,* Oliver and Boyd, Edinburgh and London, 1959, p. 126.

in which our economy functions. It has tried negating the effects of a changing field by imposing a prescribed behavior on individual particles in that field. It cannot be done – no more than an electro-magnetic field can be significantly changed by working on a single charge found in it.

No commodity can be considered *in vacuo,* either with regard to its price, its supply or its demand. Only with the greatest reservations can comparisons be made between the price of a loaf of bread in the same country at distant points of time.

To set up our economic field we must seek in the real world the influences that are critical to the economy; and we must consider the exact manner of their interaction. If they originate in distinct social areas and answer distinct laws, that must be expressed in our theory. Mathematical tools must be brought in only when we have determined the structures of reality.

This far from a simple task. It is not surprising, therefore, that even the greatest economic thinkers should have contributed to our fiascoes. Their achievements in plotting one socio-economic field successfully was no guarantee of their success when they turned their attention elsewhere.

It tells us much about the weird ways of the human mind that for the most penetrating analysis of capitalism we must go to the writings of Karl Marx, while it is the champions of the free market like Hayek who provide us with the best insights into the distribution problems of socialism.

When Marx approached capitalist production, he did so as a scientist; when he came to socialism he turned visionary. The nexus between his analysis of capitalism and his views on socialism is the sheerest banana peel. He did not even pose the problems that beset the socialist economies of our day. On the other hand, the marginal theoreticians treat the market like true believers; their scientific acumen they reserve for their criticism of socialism.

Only in our day are the most perspicacious academic economists of the West discovering some of the basic traits of capitalism that were analysed by Marx over a century ago. Painfully, belatedly, and with a touching innocence of the vast literature on these matters long grown yellow, our economists are discovering what capitalism was about.

There was already, of course, more than a touch of irony when Keynes solved the riddle of inadequate demand in the thirties – a phenomenon that socialists had been talking about at the top of their voices for a century and marginalist doctrine had claimed could not exist. Unfortunately Keynes – ever the esthete – wanted both to smash his ikons and keep them. He circumvented rather than challenged the dogma that marginal theory had built into its idiom.

Not so long ago G. L. S. Shackle came up with the long neglected key to Keyne's view of the market economy.[12] 'Keynes spares his readers, even in the deliberately provocative *General Theory of* 1936, the ultimate force of his conclusion, that rational conduct is an illusion'. . . .'The final smashing of the ideal was reserved for his last version of the theory of unemployment, the *Quarterly Journal* reply to his critics. . . . His summary statement, uttered in speech was "Equilibrium is blither".' . . . 'The *General Theory,* if we see it in the light of Keynes's final recognition of his own meaning . . . was an Economics of Disorder. The analysis of business life as a steady application of reason to changeable, but knowable and coherent circumstances, the analysis of business conduct as an informed, collected, undismayed response to a stream of understandable and largely foreseeable events was destroyed, rejected, overthrown in ruin and contempt.'

In brief, thirty-five years after the *General Theory,* one of the most perceptive of Keynes's followers has finally worked his way to Marx's 'anarchy of capitalist production'.

And yet a sardonic tribute goes with the recognition of basic truths with the time-lag of a century: when finally revealed the truths are likely to have lost some of their validity.

Our economy today is not the same as it was when Marx made his analysis. What was capitalism has evolved into a mixed economy with complex interactions between the market and non-market sectors. In significant degree price movement is determined by structural influences originating outside the market. And to foretell price movement it is often enough to observe what is happening in the *non-market areas.* Into the anarchy of the capitalist market, our mixed economy has introduced some broad certainties. If we are looking through the right end of the telescope and consulting the proper charts, we can make out

12 *Epistemics and Economics – a Critique of Economic Doctrines,* Cambridge University Press, 1972, pp. 233 and 429.

Shackle stops short of disengaging himself completely from the preconceptions of equilibrium theory by identifying 'rational conduct' with the specific maximizing logic of marginal theory. There is, of course, an ambiguity in the very term 'rational': it can be taken to mean 'conforming to a law and hence predictable', or, alternately 'making sense from the viewpoint of the transactor's interest'. In the first sense the rush of lemmings into the sea would be perfectly rational conduct.

some headlands through the old, pea-soup mists.[13]

We are able, in short, to note changes in the socio-economic field in which market activities take place. It is no longer enough to divide our analysis into micro-economic and macro-economic – the economics of the individual firms and that of the entire market economy. In addition we must direct our attention to *social macro-profiles,* to those structural changes in society at large that influence the economic field. If we fail to do so, a macro-economic statistic or concept may prove a false aggregate that blinds us to critical new structures in the economy.

Thus if the public sector has undergone rapid growth in the economy, we can predict a rising price trend. Inevitably a growing layer of taxation must seep into price to pay for this; in relative terms the tax base will have narrowed and the burden of public services supported by it will have increased. Elsewhere I have called this layer of taxation in price the *social lien* and studied its laws in some detail.[14]

Or if we should have a levelling-out of living standards imposed by legislation or other non-market agents, we may know in advance that there will be a further contribution to structural price rise. I have called such factors *social revalorization.*

We can trace the feedback loops of such structural factors in their action upon one another, as well as the responses they elicit on the market. But to make use of such readily available information, our perceptions must be suitably structured by our theory. As things stand, however, the symbolism of marginal theory stands as a screen between economists and the most obvious relationships in our mixed economy. It has shut their eyes to elements of predictability where these do exist, and led them to seek such predictability where it cannot possibly be found – in the anarchy of the market.

That emerges clearly from the record of the attempts to stabilize prices over the past decade. The minds of the policy-makers were dominated by the trade-cycle pattern of an earlier age. There was in

13 The Greek 'chaos', via the Flemish, gave rise to our word 'gas'. And the behavior of the individual gas molecule is, indeed, chaotic — it can only be described statistically. Nonethless, the bulk behavior of gases under *external* influence is perfectly predictable. Indeed, observation of the effects on gases of changes in pressure, volume, and temperature enabled physicists to formulate some of the earliest laws of their science.

So, too, with the chaos of the market in a mixed economy. Certain market trends can be foretold from the boundary conditions imposed upon it by the structural changes taking place outside the market.

14 Krehm op. cit. pp. 47 et seq. For social revalorization p. 99.

all of this, too, a touch of the fire and brimstone of the fundamentalist preacher: if we allowed creeping inflation to go on, we would be overtaken by the fate of Germany after World War One. . . .

. . . In its famous beer-halls at the time of the patrons learned to order several mugs of beer at once: they were content to drink it tepid rather than risk buying it by the single mug, for between mugs the price would double. And since surely nobody would want to drink his beer tepid, ergo. . . .

There were, however, a few special circumstances surrounding that celebrated German hyperinflation that are usually omitted in the telling – the impossible reparations the Allies tried extracting from the prostrate German economy, the French occupation of the Ruhr, the national strike proclaimed against it.

Moreover, this sudden concern for history on the part of a discipline guided by a super-historical model is in itself somewhat suspect.

There is after all a great deal more to history than the German inflation of the early twenties. In recent decades a new discipline of the history of prices has arisen. It has sought to piece together the fragmentary record of prices in Europe from the Middle Ages. What have been its findings? Has it managed to detect a trend towards price equilibrium that might justify the equilibrium model of conventional theory? By no means. There has been an almost uninterrupted price climb over the centuries. Jean Fourastié sums up the French record as follows: 'If all these prices do indeed obey a simple law, I have not noticed it; to the best of my knowledge these prices do not have laws so much as a *history*. . . . . Yet that does not mean that they do not show certain tendencies, certain influences. . . .'[15]

The reason for this is that prices are formed in an ever-changing field of social and economic relationships. Their movement can only be understood with reference to that field. All this was far too complex for the early economists to build their theories on. Instead, many of them took as their benchmark the precious metals. But here again we are dealing with anything but stable units. In an age of daring explorations and evolving technique, the supply and cost of the precious metals were subject to violent shifts. They were, nonetheless, palpable substances with far-sung properties; they had been invested with symbolic attributes from the earliest times. It was thus unavoidable that they should have been impressed into service to provide all too simple

15 *L'Evolution des prix à long terme, ouvrage publié sous la direction de Jean Fourastié,* Paris, Presses Universitaires de France, 1969, pp. 30, 87 and 75.

explanations for quite complex social phenomena. This practice goes on right to our own day: central bankers sagely examine their M-1 and M-2 money figures to see how we are doing at 'licking inflation' – very much as Rome's priests used to read the future from studying the entrails of the sacrificial victims.

Again the quantity theory of money upon which this practice is based is supported by a highly selective pinch of misinterpreted history. In freshman economics courses students are still taught about the influx of American gold having caused the price surge of the 16th century. Years ago price historians exploded that version. Summarizing their conclusions. René Grandamy has this to say: 'The traditional explanation of the Price Revolution comes up against some serious difficulties – the price rise in Europe seems clearly to have begun before 1525, or more than twenty years before the discovery of the Potosí deposits (1545), and thus about twenty-five years before the massive imports of silver. . . . Moreover, the classic explanation of price rise by referring to the influx of metallic silver does not explain why salaries remained stable.

'We can only conclude that between the 15th and 17th century *the balance of the food supply* was upset. This led to a sharp decline in the living standards of wage-earners and a monstrous increase in the revenues of landed proprietors.'[16]

Grandamy goes on to list a series of economic dislocations that resulted from the demographic pressure on food supply: the cultivation of less fertile lands worked intensively by laborers whose living standards dropped to make this possible; the reorientation of secondary and tertiary activities to cater to the needs of the rich; the breaking up of family farms, the changed relationship of city and countryside. Innumerable historians of price and economic historians concur in these conclusions. They reveal to us a complete remaking of the socio-economic field in 16th and 17th-century Europe. Economists ignore all this. They go on citing the Price Revolution of the sixteenth century as justification for what they are wreaking upon our economics in the late twentieth.

The period that would seem to come closest to providing a historical basis for the model of price equilibrium is the nineteenth century. But that, too, is deceptive. A variety of circumstances joined to create a gently sinking price level.

The spread of the industrial system to the continent undermined

16 Jean Fourastié ed., op. cit. pp. 154-7 and 332.

Britain's monopoly in the field. The opening up of the pampas of the New World brought to Europe a flood of cheap food. And while technological revolution reduced the price of industrial goods, the development depended largely on improved physical factors. The labor force continued barely literate. It imposed little burden on the state for its care or education. In the absence of trade unions its aspirations were rudimentary. It was, moreover, a period of protracted peace in Europe: state expenditure sank as a proportion of the national income. And during these years there was a progressive shift to the gold standard that had a depressant effect on price.

It was a weakness of the nineteenth century to mistake the local scenery for God-ordained universal laws. Relative price stability, the resultant of a welter of chance circumstances, came to be taken as a norm. And in our day economists have simply skipped over the exercise of enquiring to what extent stable price is possible in a mixed economy, and by grace of what relationships.

The answer to that neglected question appears clearly in the disastrous record of price stabilization policy over the past fifteen years. Central to the entire curious experience is the assumption that upward price movement is *per se* pathological. It is dealt with like a case of measles; there is no question of the patient being allowed to go about his normal business 'until inflation has been licked'.

The therapy deals less with symptoms than with prepackaged syndromes. In our pluralistic economy all sorts of unexplored circuits connect public expenditure with costs and price. Inevitably these trigger different multipliers and feedbacks; for price is very much the nervous system of a market economy. Our therapists, however, are content to reason concerning the problems of this complex economy in terms of a simplistic model: if prices go up, it can only be that there is too much demand even though industrial plant is visibly idle. The system is 'overheated' and has to be 'cooled' – i.e. it must be deflated by punitive interest rates, credit restrictions, and increased taxes. In almost every instance when this was done the price climb persisted, and even took on new momentum. And for those who had eyes to see, the reason was obvious enough.

Our modern economy operates under an increasingly costly overhead. Contributing to this are not only the physical plant and infrastructures needed to run a modern society, but the human capital that has become the major part of our national investment. An unemployed engineer tends to rust quite as much as unused railway track – and the cost to society of that sort of rust is far greater. In 1969 Sir Roy Harrod formulated what has come to be known as the 'Harrod dichotomy' – 'when aggregate demand is below the supply potential a reduction of demand will raise real unit costs . . . and therefore have a price-inflationary tendency'.[17]

That, however, is only part of the story; the concept must be extended. In a pluralistic society the employers are no longer entirely quit of labor costs when they shut down their plants for lack of orders. Labor power is no longer bought by the piece as in Marx's day. The unemployed and the problems they develop during their forced unemployment are a burden on the state, and that ultimately, through taxes, finds its way back to the private sector as an added cost.

The importance of this expanded 'Harrod dichotomy' will vary from country to country, depending upon the relative costliness of their physical and social 'overhead'. A classic illustration is provided by Canada. It was strung together against the natural grain of the continent from sparsely settled pockets separated by thousands of miles of barren rock – a rosary of political faith with more string than beads. This in itself results in a far higher proportion of public sector to private sector, and an abnormally high proportion of social lien in the Canadian price structure. To this must be added the higher administration costs of running a quasi-bilingual society, and the mediocrity of the economies of scale even when the economy is running at capacity. Deflating that economy 'to lick inflation' is accordingly bound to push prices far higher than similar policies would do in the United States. It is certain to disadvantage Canada's position as exporter, as a rule a subject of vocal concern on the part of Canadian price-stabilizers. Experience has repeatedly confirmed this very obvious analysis. And yet the professional corps of 'inflation fighters' has never chosen to acknowledge the relationship.

When the patient's symptoms refuse to yield to the healers' science, tempers become frayed. The Invisible Hand becomes highly visible, complete with knuckle-dusters. The doctors announce that they will not wince at the sight of blood: it does not matter what unemployment might result in the 'trade-off', prices have to be stabilized. The patient in this way ends up with both the cure and the disease.

After this has gone on long enough, the politicians, more alert to realities than their economic advisers, usually decide that the economy

---

17 Letter to The Economist, July 19th, 1969.

must be allowed to recover. But not for long. As the economic recovery lessens the political pressures, the stabilizers step to the fore again. As a result what used to be more or less a 7-year cycle, visited upon the world by faceless gods, has become a 1-year affair inflicted by the policy-makers. There are times when the permitted recovery and the new dosage of deflation have occurred within the one calendar year.[18]

---

18 'I'm afraid . . . that there are a lot of people in this country who are bargaining that . . . the Government can't act tough for long because it will only get frightened if it sees unemployment up to 6%. If people think that we are going to lose our nerve because of that, they should think again'. Prime Minister Pierre E. Trudeau, quoted in the Canadian edition of *Time,* January 12, 1970. At the time of this writing unemployment in Canada is in excess of 8%, and the rate of price increase is currently at an annual rate of over 8% in spite of two years of price controls under the Anti-Inflation Board.

A perusal of the press of a decade ago will produce samples of economic reporting that might be coming out of our capitals today—with a single discrepancy: the rate of 'unacceptable inflation' that stirred the stabilizers into action then would be hailed as a blessing today.

'Only six months ago, the U.S. economy was heating rapidly and Lyndon Johnson decided to cool it. . . . He asked Congress for a temporary suspension of the 7% investment tax credit on plant and equipment spending. The move helped chill the economy so much that last week the President requested Congress to reinstate the credit nine months ahead of schedule.' *(Time,* March 17th, 1967).

Washington's economic experts were casting themselves in the role of short-order cooks, but without happy results. What they tried heating turned out cold cuts; and what they undertook to cool burned in the pan.

'In a move that most moneymen had not expected for weeks or even months, the Federal Reserve Board lowered its discount from 5½% to 5¼%. . . . Unless the credit brakes were eased, so their argument ran, the combination of both fiscal and monetary restraint could slow the economy too much and create the risk of mini-recession . . . despite a huge backlog of unfilled demand for new housing, the result of the 1966 credit squeeze that crippled the industry for a year'. *(Time,* August 23rd, 1968). Two weeks later the same magazine reported: 'In June and July, the cost of living made its steepest two-month climb in eleven years.'

The very language took on a martial tone. 'For its part the Federal Reserve Board will have to avoid the stop-and-go policies that in the past have produced sharp, erratic swings in the money supply. . . . One of the Federal Reserve's seven governors puts it "we mean business in breaking the inflationary psychology".

Soon we were treated to body-counts as an index of progress. The bulletins from this theater developed a style strangely reminiscent of those from other fronts: there were the same confident schedules, boldly announced and then quietly forgotten, the same escalation of forces. And no matter how victorious the action, the enemy had a way of turning up in

After many rounds of such counterproductive policy, of misfired forecast and hopeless bungling, it becomes apparent to the most trusting citizen that in their stabilization efforts our governments do not know what they are about. At that point secondary symptoms develop that give off an unmistakable odor of social decomposition. A theory that has the word 'rational' ever on its lips, has contributed to a surge of unreasoning conduct that threatens to overwhelm our society.

This it has achieved by advancing the promise of price stability where stable prices are ruled out. When reality gives the lie to the vision, the only possible conclusion is that villainy is somewhere afoot. That is a dangerous format for thinking on public matters; it activates primitive resonances.

Early man's loyalties were fiercely tribal, and they were given added coherence by the rejection of the outlander. In some respects this contributed to a psychic balance: aggressive impulses could be safely disposed of outside the tribe. The last few centuries, however, have seen a rapid expansion of the area of communal loyalties. Cities and feudal fiefs gave way to nations, and with the national state so patently obsolescent in so many respects, humanity has been groping towards more comprehensive solidarities. These extended allegiances,

---

greater strength behind the lines.

'Last week the Commerce Department reported that its index of leading indicators . . . rose sharply in April. The Labor Department estimated that wholesale prices jumped at an estimated annual rate of 7.2% in May up from 2.4% in April. Such figures only sharpen the debate about whether the Federal Reserve and the Nixon Administration are fighting inflation hard enough – or too hard. . . . Some moneyman believe that the government is risking "overkill"; others agree that it has to do just that.' (*Time,* June 6th, 1969).

In the *Economic Report of the President* of February, 1971 (United States Government Printing Office, p. 60) we read: 'Though the reasons for the stubborness of the inflation in 1970 are not fully clear, two main explanations are usually offered. . . . One relates to the duration and magnitude of the preceding inflationary boom. . . . The other would trace the cause to structural changes in the economic system. . . . Various observers with different viewpoints are impressed with the apparently irresistible agglomerations of power represented by large corporations and unions.'

In the megalithic, bureaucratic jungle that is Washington, the economic advisers scanned the horizon for structural changes in the economy, and the only things they could come up with was 'the power represented by large corporations and unions.'

Like ancient Thebes, we rely for guidance upon blind seers.

however, place a strain on modern man. He is left without a safe disposal ground for his aggressive feelings – it is rather like the problem of our monstrous cities in finding dumping grounds for their noxious wastes.

When in this context economists advance a theory that is an invitation to endless recrimination, they are disturbing dangerous ground. Society is encouraged to personify its problems. That not only provides instant emotional release; it spares us the mental exertion of trying to understand them. And from there on the whole process picks up mindless momentum. Anything that harms the villain is by definition good. It is like enlisting in a wartime army. You no longer need trouble your head about rights and wrongs. When a certain color of uniform appears before you, you shoot.

At bottom what happened is that our social accountancy has broken down. The failure of economic theory has undermined the possibility of bargaining between group and group, indeed even of meaningful communication. In a world that needs batteries of computers to keep track of its affairs, we find ourselves without a reliable unit of reckoning. A dimension has been added to society's alienation.

Chapter Two

Descent Into Metaphysics

What is disturbing about our economic theory is not that its has been wrong – it is after all a human science. It is rather that being an all too human effort, it has arrogated to itself quite godly attributes. And as a result it has locked itself in its error and thrown the key away. By the empirical principles that it claims to hold dear, its misfired predictions and policy disasters should long ago have led to correctives. They have not. The theory persists like the nagging idiocy of a phonograph needle caught in a damaged groove.

A spurious empiricism somehow shuts off our economists' view of reality. Ours is an age in which quatification has come to fill the niches once occupied by the saints. Mention a statistic baptised in printer's ink and your educated citizen glows with the reassuring feeling that he is dealing with solid facts. The manner in which that statistic has been produced and the validity of the concept behind it are rarely questioned. Nevertheless such uncritical worship of 'facts' can befuddle our thinking as much as any transcendental mysticism.[1]

---

1 'The single comprehensive GNP figure is made up of factors (capital goods, government services, military expenditures, etc.) which have widely differing meanings in diverse national contexts, and affect human welfare in uncertain ways according to individual tastes and desires. The conclusion is that even when two countries have the same GNP, say £100 Mn this identical figure may hide varying material and welfare standards in the two countries. . . . But the public knows of course nothing about these reservations when they are sold some dose of government intervention on the basis of a single GNP figure. . . . Some (academic economists) write popular articles and speak in plain language on the BBC about economic matters; the nature of the mass media permits them to mention GNP growth rates and numerate forecasts, but of course denies them the opportunity to introduce the qualifying reservations they would ordinary make to academic audiences. Such behaviour constitutes misrepresentation.' (Alex Rubner, *Three Sacred Cows of Economics*, Macgibbon & Kee, London, 1970, p. 16.)

Close to the root of all this is the peculiar empiricist tradition in the Anglo-Saxon world. And since in economic theory, the English-speaking countries enjoy something like a right of primogeniture, the effects of this have been felt internationally. An immense amount of analysis of great refinement has been carried on by British and American economists; but both the point of departure and inference from most of this has been that the common good is best served by leaving matters to the unobstructed wisdom of the markets: over these a benign providence keeps watch under a variety of aliases ('The Invisible Hand', the equilibrium points of Walras's equations, and so forth). For practical purposes, this sort of theory has been self-liquidating. Its belief in the self-balancing features of the economy afforded as stylized an exit from the stage of action as any act of hara-kiri did in the Japanese theater. A weird symbiosis set in between a narrowly empirical practice and a pretentious if gelded system of analysis.

In North America the Yankee tinker archetype contributed to the cleavage between analysis and practice.[2] The legendary example of this was Henry Ford who revolutionized production while taking no pains to hide his contempt for abstract thinking. If by a more circuitous route, the neo-Keynesian models that have flourished in America also arrived at Ford's unforgettable conclusion: 'History is bunk'. Since economic activity in their paradigm unfolds according to superhistorical principles, it could have little relevance to the workaday world which, after all, is history in the making.

Times there were when such idealized empiricism was an asset. These were the eras when the world was pretty much the oyster first of Britain and then of the United States. In such a situation what was needed was less a theory than an appetite. Today that is no longer the case. We use the expression 'mixed economy' glibly, but rarely pause to consider that this implies that our economy is no longer governed by a single code. Certainly the rarefied model of the private sector is not remotely to be identified with what goes on in our world today. We have need of our full powers of analysis to understand the new patterns taking shape around us.

The empiricist tradition stands in the way of our doing this. There is an abiding superstition that whatever is not facts and figures is bound to be a waste of time. We find even Joan Robinson, one of the great

---

2 Note in this connection the popularity of the expression 'toolbox' in American economic literature.

economists of our time, dismissing all value theories as 'metaphysics'.[3] Properly understood, metaphysics is, however, precisely what economists stand in need of – a fundamental rethinking of the relationship of our minds to the reality around us.

There is to begin with the superstition that facts are out there indisputable and ready-made; and that all we have to do is lasso them and bring them home as cowboys do with cattle on the range. The philosophers of symbolism have shown, however, that what we consider 'facts' are very much the products of structures that have taken possession of our thinking. It is these that determine what we can and what we cannot perceive. For economists, imprisoned as they are in concepts that have nothing to do with our economic reality, the point is important enough to dwell upon. It is ironic that a discipline that has attempted to ride on the coat-tails of 18th century physics should have paid so little heed to what has been happening in that science in more recent years.

Suzanne Langer has written: 'Genuine empiricism is above all a reflection on the validity of sense-knowledge, a speculation on the ways our concepts and beliefs are built out of the fleeting and disconnected reports our eyes and ears actually make to the mind. Positivism, the scientists' metaphysic, entertains no such doubts, and raises no epistemological problems; its belief in the veracity of sense is implicit and dogmatic. . . . It repudiates the basic problems of epistemology, and creates nothing but elbow-room for laboratory work. The very fact that it rejects *problems,* not answers, shows that the growing physical sciences were geared to an entirely different outlook on reality.. They had their own so-called "working notions", and the strangest of these was the concept of *fact.*' . . . 'An undisputed and uncritical empiricism — not skeptical, but positivistic – became the official metaphysical creed, experiment its avowed method, a vast hoard of "data" its capital, and correct prediction of future occurrences its proof.'[4]

Such was last-century positivism, the philosophy of science of that day. But in our century physics has been wracked by the very metaphysical problems that positivism was supposed to have eliminated forever. 'The faith of scientists in the power and truth of mathematics is so implicit that their work has gradually become less and less observation, and more and more calculation. The promiscuous collection and tabulation of data have given way to a process of assigning possible

3 *Economic Philosophy,* Chicago, Aldine Publishing Co., 1962, pp. 7-9.
4 *Philosophy in a New* Key, Mentor Books, New York, 1948 pp. 24, 28.

meanings, merely supposed real entities, to mathematical terms, working out the logical results, and then staging certain crucial experiments to check the hypothesis against the actual, empirical results. . . . With the advance of mathematical techniques in physics, the tangible results of experiment have become less and less spectacular; on the other hand, their significance has grown in inverse proportion. . . . Observation has become almost entirely indirect; and *readings* take the place of genuine witness. The sense-data on which the propositions of modern science rest are, for the most part, little photographic spots and blurs, or inky curved lines on paper. . . . What is directly observed is only a sign of the "physical fact"; it requires interpretations to yield scientific propositions. . . . The problem of observation is all but eclipsed by the problem of *meaning*. And the triumph of empiricism in science is jeopardized by the surprising truth that our *sense-date are primarily symbols.'*

Of crucial importance in all this is the distinction between signs and symbols. 'The logical relation between a sign and its object is a very simple one: they are associated, somehow, to form a pair; that is to say they stand in a one-to-one correlation. To each sign there corresponds one definite item which is its object, the thing . . . signified.

'The interpretation of signs is the basis of animal intelligence. Animals presumably do not distinguish between natural signs and artificial or fortuitous signs. They use both kinds to guide their practical activities. We do the same thing all day long. We answer bells, watch the clock, obey warning signals, follow arrows. . . . Because a sign may mean so many things, we are very apt to misinterpret it. . . . Wet streets are not a reliable sign of recent rain if the sprinkler wagon has passed by. . . .'

The reader will have no difficulty in recognizing here the structural principle that underlies most of the deductions of conventional economic theory – the 'trade-offs' of unemployment for greater price stability; inflation due to an excess of money supply; higher prices signifying an excess of demand, and so forth. We are in strictly Pavlovian territory.

Symbols are something else again. 'Symbols are not proxy for their objects, but are *vehicles for the conception of objects*. . . . In talking *about* things we have conceptions of them, not the things themselves; and it is the conceptions, not the things, that symbols "mean".

'Propositional structure has commanded more interest among logicians of the present generation than any other aspect of symbolism. Ever since Bertrand Russell *(A Critical Exposition of the Philosophy of*

Leibniz (1900), p. 12) pointed out that the Aristotelian metaphysics of substance and attribute is a counterpart of the Aristotelian logic of subject and predicate – that the common-sense view of things and properties, agents and patient, object and action, etc. is a faithful counterpart of the common-sense logic embodied in our parts of *speech* – the ties between expressibility and conceivability, forms of language and forms of experience, propositions and facts, have been drawn closer and closer. . . . A proposition is a picture of a structure – the structure of a state of affairs.' [5]

We shall be misled if we assume that we are somehow dealing with absolutely valid 'facts', rather than certain aspects of reality perceived through the structures of language and theory. Ernst Cassirer has shown how easily we can slip back into more primitive thinking patterns founded on just such assumptions.[6] 'According to Hume every representation of causality should ultimately be derived from the representation of mere coexistence. Two contents which have appeared together

5 An exact parallel developed in pure mathematics with the recognition that every associative algebra is the equivalent of a matric algebra. 'The essential point in the proof of this equivalence, i.e. the variables can be replaced by the transformational structures linking one set of variables to another, is brought out most naturally by explaining the correspondence, first noted by Poincaré, between the elements of any associative algebra A over a field D and the linear transformations of a certain set'. (Leonard Eugene Dickson, *Algebras and their Arithmetics,* Dover Publications, Inc., New York, 1960, p. 62).

The very speech in which we communicate consists in large degree of such structures of transformation. 'Where a precise world is lacking to designate the novelty which the speaker would point out he resorts to the powers of *logical analogy and uses a word denoting something else that is a presentational symbol for the thing he means:* the context makes it clear that he cannot mean the thing literally denoted, and must mean something else symbolically. . . . If he says "the king's anger flares up", we know from the context that "flaring up" cannot refer to the sudden appearance of a physical flame. . . .

'Wegner (Philip Wegener, *Untersuchungen ueber die Grundfragen des sprachlebens)* calls such a word a "faded metaphor", and shows . . . that all general words are probably derived from specific appelations, by metaphorical use; so that our literal language is a very repository of "faded metaphors" ' (Langer, op. cit. p. 123).

Our speech and thinking is then carried on in terms of structural matrices quite as much as the calculations of quantum mechanics. Like Molière's hero who has spoken prose all his life, however, we are unconscious of the fact.

6 *The Philosophy of Symbolic Forms,* Vol. 2, *Mythical Thought,* translated by Ralph Manheim, Yale University Press, New Haven and London, 1964, pp. 44 et seq.

in consciousness with sufficient frequency are ultimately transposed, through the mediating psychological function of "imagination", from a relationship of mere contiguity, of mere spacial coexistence or temporal succession, into a causal relation. But in truth, scientific knowledge gains its causal concepts and judgments by an exactly opposite process. Through these concepts and judgments contents which are contiguous for immediate sensory impressions are progressively dissected and assigned to different complexes of conditions. In mere perception a specific state A in moment A_1 is followed by another B in moment A_2. But regardless of how often it is repeated, this succession would not lead to the idea that A is the "cause" of B – the *post hoc* would never become a *propter hoc* – unless a mediating concept intervened. From the state A thought isolates a specific factor α which it links with factor β in B. That α and β stand in a necessary relation to each other, a relation of "cause" and "effect", of "condition" and "conditioned", is not passively read from a given perception or number of perceptions: . . . Particularly the physical *experiment* on which causal judgments in physics finally depend is always based on such analysis of an occurrence into different spheres of conditions, different strata of relations'.

Scientists, in fact, seek out the matrices of causal relationships, and direct their primary interest to these.

'This isolating abstraction, which singles out a specific factor in a total complex as a "condition", is alien to mythical thinking. Here every simultaneity, every spatial coexistence and contact, provide a real causal "sequence". It has even been called a principle of mythical causality and of the "physics" based on it that one take every contact in time and space as an immediate relation of cause and effect. The principle of *post hoc, ergo propter hoc* and *juxta hoc, ergo propter hoc* are characteristic of mythical thinking. Animals appear in a certain season are, for example, commonly looked upon as the bringers, the cause of the season.'

To show how pertinent all this is to our problems of economic theory, I shall quote from a recent book of John H. Hotson, *Stagflation and the Bastard Keynesians* (p. 54): 'the relationship of money and prices is often expressed in the form of the "Equation of Exchange (EOE) developed by Irving Fisher: $MV \equiv PT$, where M represents the stock of money, and V is the rate of turn-over. The triple bar states that M times V is identically equal to P times T, where P is the price level and T is the volume of money transactions. If, in the short run, the volume of transaction is fixed by the amount of production, employment, and exchange people are engaged in, and V is fixed by payment habits and contracts requiring payment at fixed intervals, it must follow by mathematical necessity that M and P are directly proportional to each other. This, in itself, is not a "quantity of money theory of the price level", as distinguished from a "price-level theory of the quantity of money". However, the essence of monetarism is the belief in "left to right" causality, the belief that by and large an increase in the money supply causes a rise in the price level rather than the reverse.

'Since the rise of national income accounting, it is customary to express the equation of exchange as $MV \equiv PQ$, where Q represents real, or constant purchasing power dollar income and output, and PQ is the current dollar value of the output, thus Gross National Product, GNP. . . .

'The remaining theories of inflation we wish to consider can likewise be expressed as truisms. Thus we may write: $MV \equiv PQ \equiv GNP \equiv C+I+G + (X-m) \equiv kW \equiv hB \equiv DPY + DGY + DFY \equiv jS$. Our new terms express tht GNP is identical to the sum of Consumption (C), Investment (I), Government Expenditures (G), and Exports (X) less Imports (m). GNP is also identical to some multiple (k) of the Wage Bill (W). It is also identical to some decimal of Total Net Debt (B), and the sum of Disposable Personal Income (DPY), Disposable Business Income (DBY), Disposable Government Income (DGY), and Disposable Foreign Income (DBY). . . . Finally, GNP is identical to some very large multiple (j) of my salary (S). Each of these identities may be expressed as a price level equation by dividing through by Q, thus with rearrangement we have:
$P \equiv V(M/Q) \equiv GNP/Q \equiv C+I+G+(X-m)/Q \equiv k(W/Q) \equiv h(B/Q) \equiv j(S/Q)$. It will be recognized that each of the expression to the right of an identity sign is merely an alternative definition of the price level. However, each expression may also be considered to be a causality statement. Thus. the first, or equation of exchange, states that the price level is caused by the ratio of money to real goods (times velocity) and will change as this ratio changes (unless the velocity varies). Skipping over the second term we come to its expansion in the third or "excess demand" expression, that the price level will rise whenever the sum of expenditures on Consumption, Government and the foreign balance exceed the real output of the economy. Next we have the "Wage Cost Mark-up" explaining the price level as the ratio of the wage bill to real output (times k, or "mark-up"). Next we have the "excess debt" explanation and finally we "explain" the price level as

the ratio between my salary and real output times j. Now, all these statements are equally true, but they are not equally plausible as "right to left" causality statements.'

In short Hotson is playing spoil-sport and messing up a perfect application of mythical causality by applying some critical logic. That does not happen too often in our economics faculties. More generally the mythological thought patterns of primitive tribesmen that we all carry within us are fortified by an uncritical reverence for the mathematical apparatus of science.

There remains, of course, the difficulty of the implied time sequence in any causal relationship. Spatial coexistence is a symmetrical relationship; cause and effect – necessarily ordered in time – constitute an asymmetrical relationship. Equilibrium theory, however, has gotten around that little difficulty with elegance. Let us listen to Alfred Marshall on the point: 'It is necessary to face the difficulty of regarding the various elements of an economic problem – not as determining one another in a chain of causation, A determining B, B determining C, and so on – but as all mutually determining one another.'[7] Time is thus flattened out by positing equilibrium centers around which economic events oscillate – just as a pendulum does under the joint influence of its constraint and gravitation. When it has swung too far in one direction, it is drawn back to describe a symmetrical arc in the opposite sense. In this way we not only stick close to our center of equilibrium, but no less significantly to the fundamental pattern of mythological thought.

Let us turn to Cassirer for yet another basic feature of mythic thought.[8] '. . . the mythical concept of the attribute is most evident in the structure of alchemy. . . . Here every similarity in the sensuous manifestation of different things or in their mode of action is ultimately explained by the supposition that one and the same material cause is in some way "contained" in them. Alchemy, for example, looks on bodies as complexes of simple qualities from which they arise through mere aggregation. Each attribute represents a specific elementary thing, and from the sum of these elementary things the composite world, the world of empirical bodies is built. . . . The alchemist can produce the "philosopher's stone" from common quicksilver by first extracting a water, i.e. that mobile fluid element which detracts from the true perfection of the quicksilver. His next task is to "fixate" the body thus obtained, i.e. free it from its volatility by removing an airy element

7 *Principles,* Macmillan Limited, London, 1936, pp. lxxx, 58, 81, 294

8 Op. cit. Vol. 2, pp. 65, 68, and 60.

which it still contains. In the course of its history, alchemy developed this addition and subtraction of attributes into a highly ingenious and intricate system. . . . Modern science and particularly modern chemistry in the form given to it by Lavoisier succeeded in overcoming this semi-mythical alchemic concept of the attribute only by fundamentally re-forming the whole question. For modern science the "attribute' 'is not simple but highly complex; not original and elementary but derived. . . . Thus the inflammability of a body no longer implies the presence of a specific substance, *phlogiston,* but signifies its reaction to water or an acid, etc. The particular quality appears no longer as a substance but as something thoroughly contingent which, under causal analysis, dis-solves into a mesh of relations'. . . . 'Scientific thinking . . . proceeds at once synthetically and analytically. In similar contents it emphasizes the factor of dissimilarity as well as the factor of similarity. . . . When mathematical thinking subsumes the circle and the ellipse, the hyperbola and parabola under *one* concept, this subsumption is not grounded in any immediate similarity of forms, which from the standpoint of the senses are as dissimilar as possible. But in characterizing all these forms as "conic sections", mathematical thinking apprehends a unity of *law,* a unity of structural principle in the midst of dissimilarity.'

'For myth the thing is present as a whole, as soon as anything similar to it is given. In the tobacco smoke rising from a pipe the mythical consciousness sees neither a mere symbol nor a mere instrument for making rain – it sees the tangible image of a cloud and in this image the thing itself, the desired rain.'

There is a complete parallelism here with the way in which conven-tional economic theory has viewed 'inflation'. Rather than examine the various factors that contribute to price rise in their diverse relation-ships, the price climb in itself becomes the thing: by removing the attribute of climbing price without seeking its specific causes, we will be 'licking inflation'. That is why governments have pushed their economies to the brink of disaster with punitively high interest rates, credit restrictions, and systems of price control that showed no curiosity about the workings of the industries they were undertaking to control. All this was to drive out the devil, pardon, the attribute of inflation.

And yet there is no reason for despair. Cassirer regards mythic thinking as a stage in the development of a scientific view of the world. 'In this respect it may be said that each of these forms, before taking on its specific logical form and character, must pass through a pre-liminary mythical stage. The astronomical picture of the cosmos and of the articulation of bodies in the cosmos originated in the astrological view of space and of processes in space. Before the general doctrine of motion developed into a pure mechanics – a mathematical representation of the phenomena of motion – it had sought to answer the question of the source of motion, which took it back to the mythical problem of the "prime mover". . . . Long before number became a pure unit of measurement it was reversed as sacred number, and an aura of this reverence still attended the beginnings of scientific mathematics.'

In this perspective equilibrium economics could stand in the same relation to an economic science as astrology to astronomy, or alchemy to chemistry. The only difference is this: today time presses. Disciplines that were able to slough off their mystic cauls some centuries back have created problems for society that only an economic science can handle.

Chapter Three

Detour Through System Dynamics

In this chapter I shall apply to our mixed economy the method of system dynamics. This articulates the causal circuits that are observed to exist. It pays particular attention to feedback loops. 'The feedback loop is the closed path that connects an action to its effects on the surrounding conditions, and these resulting conditions in turn come back as "information" to influence further action.'[1]

The merit of this approach is that it sets aside everybody's dogma: it undertakes to 'tell things like they are'. Unfortunately in our pluralistic world 'telling things like they are' is a by no means uncomplicated exercise. In building models for the purpose we shall be making more taxing demands on our ability to free ourselves from doctrinaire preconception than on mathematical skills. That is no small matter. Mathematical skills are more readily acquired – and abused – than a grasp of social reality.

The structures that we chart in this way underly our thinking and perceptions. But when we make these structures explicit, two different things happen. Their weaknesses and limitations are revealed to the critical mind. There are also certain risks. The very uncrystallized nature of the relationships with which the mind works carries with it unlimited possibilities of association; there is about it an unending reserve of fertile ambiguities. Once we fixate the relationship in mathematical or graphic form, these alternative patterns are excluded.[2] This is, of course, a necessary step in both scientific and practical thinking; but we must never lose sight of the self-limiting nature of what we are doing. We must be prepared to retrace our steps over unburned bridges at the first indication that this is called for.

1 Jay W. Forrester, *World Dynamics,* Wright-Allen Press, Inc., Cambridge Mass., 1971, p. 17.

2 Virgilio Melchiorre, *L'Immaginazione Simbolica, Saggio de Antropologia Filosofica,* Società Il Mulino, Balogna, 1972, p. 86

SUBSYSTEM ONE – THE PURE AND PERFECT MARKET

We will use this method to plot in strip-down form the logic that underlies the self-equilibrating market model. This is at the very basis of marginal value theory in which economists are drilled to do their thinking.

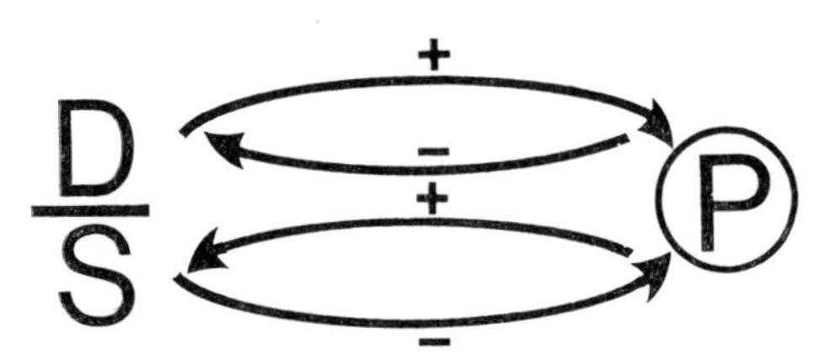

This is a feedback system, but of a peculiarly linear and monist sort. By definition supply and demand are the sole determinants of price; all price movements are accounted for entirely in terms of their relationship. For this we must posit a 'pure and perfect market' with transactors of such atomized dimension that nothing they do or leave undone individually can affect the market. They respond to the stimulus of price in a blind behavioristic way. In this age of advanced information technology, their market information – other than that conveyed by price – is zero. If price is taken to be the nervous system of the economy, it is modelled entirely on the vegetative nervous system.

Crucial to this subsystem is the ratio of Demand to Supply: D/S. Any disturbance of this ratio, whether by a change of the numerator or the denominator, must result in a price movement. And that movement will give rise to an equilibrating feedback both to the numerator and the denominator. Thus increased demand will tend to drive up price; the higher price will tend to choke off demand and stimulate supply. The second half-loop from P (Price) to S or D will be opposite in sign from that of the first half-loop. It will thus contribute to restore the original balance between S and D.

Equilibrium points are assumed to exist. To support so heroic an assumption, supply curves are taken to be concave – i.e. costs rise with increased scale of production.

Though the model is supposed to be non-normative, its strongly normative character asserts itself through a highly charged terminology – 'pure and perfect', 'false pricing', etc. By the time this contraband normativeness reaches the ears of the policy-makers, it has become transmuted into a scientific principle.

By the light of this model any price pattern that does *not* tend to equilibrium is regarded as polluted. Stabilization policies inspired by the model are essentially anti-pollution efforts.

I will include the D/S – P loop as a subsystem of our model, because it does incorporate a relationship that is valid in limited areas of the economy, *other things being equal.* Rather than an absolute norm, it must be regarded as but one of several interacting subsystems.

On the other hand, I will omit 'market imperfections' – oligopoly, monopoly, and that sort of thing – from my model for two reasons.

Firstly, there is no way of assimilating them into the model convincingly: they strike at the key mechanism of the 'pure and perfect market'. They would simply invalidate its rationale and indeed its very idiom. That is why they have featured in conventional theory as little more than a footnote, a flaw in the higher order of things.

With its *a priori* notion of equilibrium points, marginal theory knows in advance what price should be. In the real world producers arrive at their prices by adding up columns of costs. The conflict between the 'pure and perfect market' and 'imperfect' markets is really one between two contrasted arithmetical operations. In the one case cost components are supposed to be arrived at by working back from a market price established by the balance of supply and demand; in the other case it is a summation. To salvage their theory equilibrium economists classify the corner grocer as an oligopolist because he adds up his costs to establish his prices, instead of continuing to sell blindly until he just breaks even on the last unit sold.[3]

There is another reason for not including 'imperfect competition' in our model. In that way I will show that even with a 'pure and perfect

---

3 There are, of course, more serious students of market power in its relation to price movement. Gardiner C. Means and others long ago drew attention to the fact that general price movement was a composite arising from different causes. He related the very different pricing behavior in various industries to the degree of concentration existing in them. Those with most concentration tend to drop their prices far less during recessions and raise them less during periods of recovery: they are able to exercise a degree of stabilizing management over their prices and alter them less frequently. Speculators, moreover, have a far smaller effect upon price in such industries.

Means, moreover, drew attention to the fact 'that the rise in prices is a natural and necessary part of the process of recovery, (that) it is a "good thing" and deserves a separate name ('reflation'). (Gardiner C. Means, *Simultaneous Inflation and Unemployment: a Challenge to Theory and* Policy in *The Roots of Inflation, The International Crisis,* Burt Franklin & Co., Inc., N.Y., 1975, p. 8).

market', the impact upon price of the other subsystems would rule out any self-equilibrating feature in the model. By including the 'pure and perfect' subsystem with no blemishes of imperfect competition, our argument, in effect, becomes an *a fortiori* one.

When this subsystem is taken as model of the economy, it shuts out from our horizon the problems that have plagued capitalism from its beginnings. The problem of adequate demand simply cannot occur. An excess of supply automatically depresses price and brings a corrective surge of demand. By Walras's Law the market is ever cleared. To deal with the world's problems, conventional economists before Keynes simply locked themselves in a paradigm that wished these problems out of existence. With such a theory to guide it, it was inevitable that the world should have been overtaken by the crisis of the 1930's with its defences down. Only after an agonizing reexamination of the eternal truths of economic theory was Keynes able to work his way out of that bind.

SUBSYSTEM TWO (THE KEYNESIAN SUBSYSTEM)

The Keynesian subsystem can be expressed diagrammatically as follows:

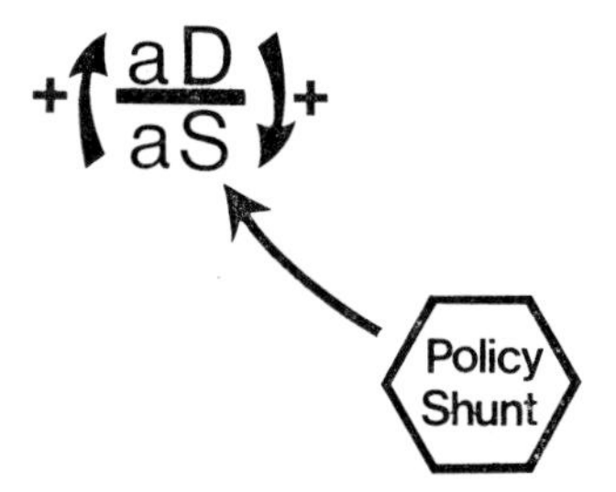

An increase in Aggregate Demand (aD) leads to an increase in Aggregate Supply (aS); an increase in aS brings on a further increase in aD, and so forth. Increased purchases arising from the greater volume of wages, materials bought, and profits from expanded production drive up demand (multiplier effect), and that increased demand stimulates a further escalation of production by triggering new investment (accelerator effect). Contrariwise, the effect will also snowball in the other direction. A decline in demand shrinks production, which further reduces demand, leading to a further curtailment of production, and so forth. A spiral pattern is established either upwards or downwards.

We have then a *divergent* feedback loop.

SUBSYSTEM 2A

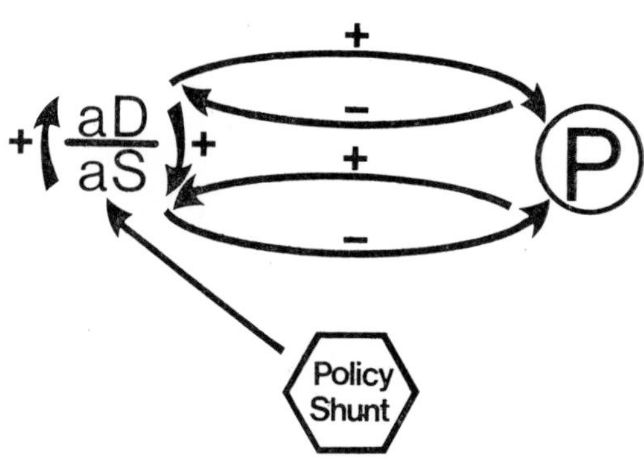

In 2A I have combined subsystems 1 and 2. It is clear from the signs of the half-loops that the result is ambiguous. Subsystem One has a self-balancing tendency because its half-loops are of inverse sign: what goes up must come down and vice versa. In Subsystem 2 the signs of the half-loops are identical. The resultant of the combined subsystems will depend upon the parameters of each and the policy input. In Subsystem 2 policy input makes its appearance. With that, the logic of the whole becomes that of a managed and not of a self-equilibrating economy.

In the combined 2A model two irreconcilable subsystems are at war – one based upon self-equilibration and the other divergent. After his brilliant job of *ad hoc* therapy, Keynes left economists attempting to reason about a non-self-equilibrating economy in an idiom – marginal theory – that was essentially self-balancing. It cannot be done. I have already quoted Keynes's mature off-the-cuff reflections on the subject as reported by Shackle.

The post-war era developed aspects that neither Keynes nor many of his contemporaries had foreseen. The public sector took on rapidly expanding importance within the economy. Keynes's work had provided the techniques to accommodate this, but its roots lay deeper. In part it could be traced to the changed social topography thrown up by the war; but basically it arose from the infrastructural needs of our new technologies. The pattern turned up no matter what the ideology of the local government. The economy that we have today calls for a more highly educated labor force, and even more educated consumers. This contributed to an explosive expansion of public education. Demographic trends added further to the role of the public sector.

In the debate that has flared forth concerning the responsibility of governments' spending for the 'inflation' they claim to combat, a point is often lost sight of: much of the expansion of the public sector has been non-discretional. It could have been carried out wastefully or frugally, but in significant degree it simply had to take place.

This changing proportion of the public to the private sector has injected a structural component into price that conventional theory has ignored. For that theory price had but a single legitimate determinant – the balancing of supply and demand. Increased taxation, in the light of that creed, could only serve as a stabilizing influence on price, 'syphoning off excess demand'. If the market is unfavorable, the producer merely decreases his purchase of materials, his hiring of workers, and spends less on other factors making up his costs. And as a result of this decreased demand *their* prices are supposed to drop likewise. Under the spell of this model it is forgotten that the tax component in costs is not set by any market, it is not bid for, and there is no way of haggling with the tax-collector any more than with the angel of death.

If we take as the point of departure for our reasoning the changing proportions of the public and private sectors – the sectorial macroprofile of the economy – we come up with an altogether different perception. The output of the public sector is delivered according to non-market redistributional principles; but it is paid for by imposts upon the private sector and its factors. The stratum of this taxation in price – the 'social lien' – answers to a logic of its own rather than to that of the market. Even if the proportion of aggregate demand to aggregate supply were to remain constant, but a shift in the proportion of these accounted for by the public and private sectors were to take place, we should have a change in our price level. That would result from the altered ratio of taxation to tax-base.

Nor is the initial effect upon price of the social lien the entire story. Even if its patterns are no longer those of the classical capitalist market, price remains the nervous system of our economy. And anything that influences the signals transmitted through price triggers reactions in all the subsystems of our mixed economy.. If you have a green signal flashing in a railway marshalling yard, you must reckon with consequences beyond consumption of electricity to light up that signal. So, too, in our economy. When prices shift owing to the novel structural factors at work in our economy, complicated multipliers snap into action; lines are short-circuited; reactions are precipitated in the various subsystems according to their individual codes. Before we know it, economic behavior takes on patterns that cannot be related to anything in the economic textbooks. A complicated circuitry has come into being and calls for decoding. In this age of advanced communications theory, that should not be a forbidding task. And yet in order to apply ourselves to it, we must first clear our minds of the preconceptions of equilibrium theory.[4]

The Social Lien Subsystem can be set up as follows:

SUBSYSTEM THREE

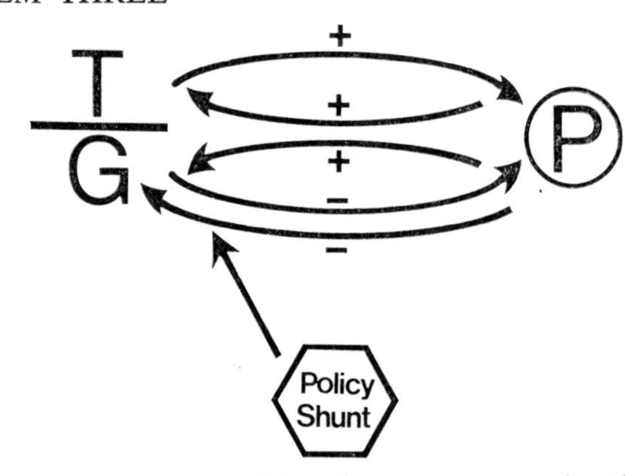

T = aggregate quantum of taxation as surrogate for the size of the public sector; G = GNP; T/G = Structural Quotient.

The causal circuit of the Social Lien Subsystem appears as two positive half-loops – T to P and back again P to T. Higher prices resulting from an increased T will tend to feed back into T positively through the higher prices of goods and salaries paid for by the state. On the other hand the same higher prices will tend to stimulate investment and thus enlarge the denominator of the crucial T/G ratio. The effect of this will be partially to restore the T/G proportion.

This ratio, which I have called the Structural Quotient, is really a surrogate for the relative magnitudes of the public sector to the entire economy. They are not quite the same because the Structural Quotient will depend not only on the relative magnitudes of the public and private sector, but on the proportion of total state spending covered out of current taxation. (Elsewhere I have gone into this matter in some detail.)[5] The Structural Quotient, though one of the most readily available and critical of statistics, was until very recently ignored by most economists.

4 Krehm, op. cit., Chapter Six.
5 Krehm, op. cit. p. 61.

By mistaking any price increase *per se* as a sign of excess demand, governments have repeatedly tried to 'lick inflation' by deflating the economy. A throttling of G through deflationary policy, however, hastens the growth of the T/G ratio by decreasing its denominator. And a deflated economy gives rise to added demand for social services at the very time that it reduces the tax-base. The Structural Quotient is thus driven up in a non-linear way.

There are other subsystems to be considered.

Our pluralistic society is busily engaged in social reorderings. The price index of any base year incorporates the economic pecking orders based upon race, sex, occupation, as they existed at the time. Legislation and institutional change, however, have removed the determination of many classes of earnings from the market rationale. This cannot but affect the price level – in a way that is not reversible by market manipulation. For example, no matter how deflated the market price of his product, the manufacturer cannot cut his costs by paying his workers less than the minimum wage, or his black workers less than his white workers. Elsewhere I have called this phenomenon Social Revalorization (SR) and analysed its multipliers.[6]

If we set up a Distribution Function $D(x_1, x_2, x_3. \ldots)$ to express the hierarchical distribution of income (i.e. distribution structured according to inherited rather than by current market influences), the element of Social Revalorization in price change will be a function of its first derivative: $SR = \emptyset\ (dD(X_1, \ldots\ldots\ldots)/dt)$.

SUBSYSTEM FOUR – SOCIAL REVALORIZATION

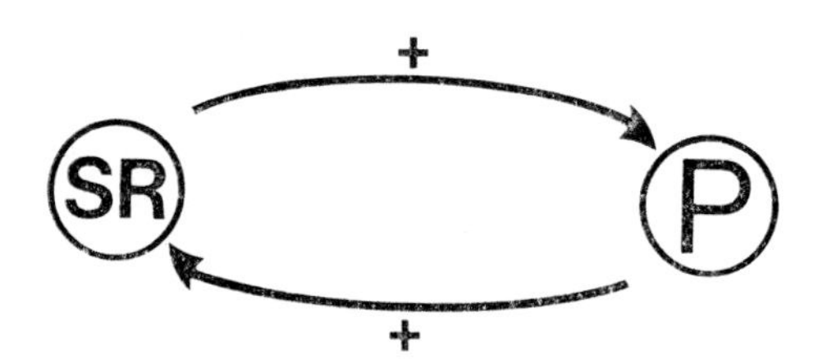

There are feedbacks in this subsystem. The latter would include Counter-Revalorization. Thus economics professors might note that garbage collectors are catching up with them in monetary earnings, and

6 Krehm, op. cit. p. 99.

might attempt to restore the historical relationship by obtaining an increase in their own salaries on such grounds.

The government, too, might try suppressing the price rise resulting from its own Social Revalorization by deflating the economy. This would add to social unrest, and escalate the SR process. The feedbacks of SR are powerfully divergent.

Another important subsystem is built around the ever larger role of services in our economy. Measurable productivity increases are concentrated largely in the mass production industries, both agricultural and and industrial. But as information acquires primacy over sheer brawn, ours is becoming a service economy. This cannot but contribute to the climb of our price indices.

To appreciate this subsystem in its true light, we must narrow the definition of the services we have in mind. For what currently passes as services in economic literature is – for our purposes – a false aggregate. It is not enough to take any transaction that does not involve the exchange of a commodity as being a service. So broad a definition would include the rental of housing and equipment, and transportation. Such exchanges are based primarily on the piecemeal consumption of physical assets; such services are capital intensive in high degree with respect to physical capital. In many instances the productivity of such services is both measurable and has increased spectacularly over recent decades – e.g. air transportation.

These are not the services relevant to our subsystem. What we refer to has to do with the primary use of human rather than physical capital – education, social services, recreational activities, information, government, therapy (though in some fields of medicine there is a strong component of physical capital as well). We would perhaps be well advised to designate such services as 'personal services' to emphasize the high proportion of human capital that goes into their production.

It is precisely such personal services that have been growing most rapidly in our economy. Employment in transportation and utilities in the United States rose by eight percent between 1947 and 1968; between 1968 and 1980 it is expected to increase by ten percent. On the other hand the corresponding figures for the increase in personal professional and business services for the same periods are 135 percent and 40 percent; for government 117 and 42.[7]

---

7 Daniel Bell, *The Coming of Post-Industrial Society,* Basic Books, Inc., N.Y., 1973, p. 131.

SUBSYSTEM FIVE – THE PERSONAL SERVICES QUOTIENT

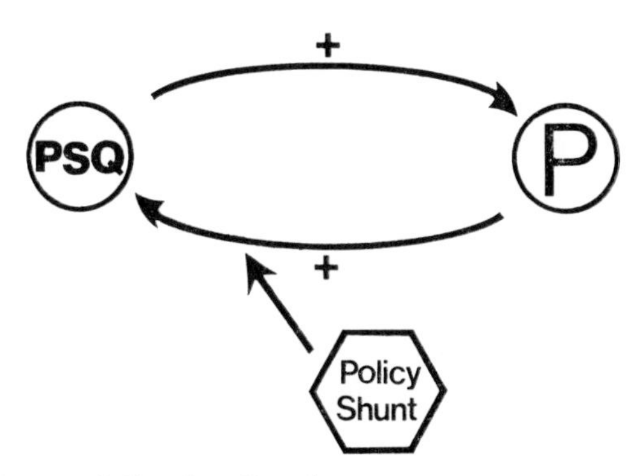

PSQ = Personal Service Quotient.

The personal services quotient (PSQ) is defined as the proportion of personal services in the national output. The substantial growth of this ratio feeds a positive input into Price. If that goes unrecognized, mistaken policy may amplify this trend. Deflationary 'stabilization' measures are more likely to throttle the manufacturing industries and further investment in them than personal services, an increasing portion of which are funded by the government. A deflated economy, moreover, calls for greater social and governmental services. Such stabilization policy would in this way accelerate the growth of the Personal Service Quotient.

For the longer term, moreover, we shall have to encourage a special type of expansion of the personal service sector in our economy. The depletion of low-cost fossil fuel and other non-renewable resources has brought the exponential growth of mass commodity production into question. Such exponential growth of the economy is, of course, implicit in the Keynesian Subsystem to provide the aggregate demand needed to keep the economy functioning. Yet given the objective constraints that we are increasingly being made aware of, more of this growth will have to be directed to services that use less non-renewable resources: educational, recreational, and cultural activities. The term 'organic growth' has been coined for such development that respects the constraints of our environment.[8]

By the logic of our Subsystem Five, this means that a growing ingredient of price rise must be fed into our price structure.

8 Mihajlo Mesarovic and Eduard Pestel, *Mankind at the Turning Point, The Second Report to the Club of Rome,* E.P. Dutton & Co., New York, 1974.

Subsystems Three, Four and Five – the Social Lien, Social Revalorization, and the Personal Services System – contribute to a price gradient. If we were to set ourselves price stability as a priority we should be depriving society of all choice concerning the quality of life. After a certain point of economic development, it is personal services rather than commodity production that determine the quality of our existence. The only way in which price would be kept stable would be through so powerfully exponential a rate of expansion in our mass production commodity sector, that its effects on price would balance the upward price pressures generated by Subsystems Three and Four and Five.

Not only would that be an unwise choice to make; it is not even open to us. It is ruled out by our Ecological and Resources Subsystem.

SUBSYSTEM SIX
THE ECOLOGICAL AND RESOURCES SUBSYSTEM

The attempts of ecologists to integrate price into their models have not been more successful than the efforts of economists to work ecological and non-renewable resource factors into theirs. On either side such issues have ignored the distinct subsystems that contribute each its specific input into price.

Howard T. Odum and Elisabeth C. Odum[9] set up a direct equivalence of monetary units and fossil-fuel energy. 'The following explanation suggests that flows of energy are a measure of value and are ultimately responsible for the values human beings attribute to money. . . . The town isolated in an agrarian region in a steady state . . . helps us understand how energy flow represents value for survival and why circulating money helps keep track of their values. . . . Money circulates from rural forms to the town and back. The money flows as a countercurrent to energy flow. It starts as low-quality energy in the country and then is transformed and concentrated by production process and the transport of product to the town. In the town, the energy is concentrated further in high-quality goods and services that are returned to the country. For a regional system to compete well and thus survive, it must use its energies in the least wasteful way while generating the most energy flow. . . . When such an energy arrangement exists, it is an equal-value loop. The circulation of money around that loop is the way human beings recognized that the flows are of equal value. The fossil-fuel equivalents of the energy flow around the loops are also equal,

9 Howard T. Odum and Elisabeth C. Odum, *Energy Basis for Man and Nature*, McGraw Hill Book Company, New York, 1976, p. 149.

since both were generated from the same energy sources. . . In steady-state conditions fossil-fuel equivalents can be used as a measure of the contribution to survival and thus to value.'

The Odums have much merit in tracking down energy flows, in emphasizing the distinction between low-quality and high-quality energies, and in developing the concept of net energy. But their excursions into social theory suffer from improvisation. Thus the circulation of money can hardly be described as 'the way human beings recognize that the flows (of energy) are of equal value'. There are societies in which money plays a quite marginal role, but energy flows effectively enough for survival. The 'steady-state' which serves as king-pin in the proof of the equivalence of energy and money is a monistic abstraction – very much the counterpart of the equilibium points of marginal theory in economics.

It is quite out of the question that our society should revert to a steady state – even if such actually existed in a remote past. We must, to be sure, balance our consumption and supply of energy. But to do this we shall have to introduce some highly dynamic changes in the structure, ethic, and motivations of our society. That implies that it will be anything but stationary, though its consumption of energy may become static or even decline. A society that has attained our level of technological development and pluralism is inescapably subject to a high momentum of change. That change must be repatterned so that we do not destroy our ecology and ourselves; but that will call for 'organic growth' rather than a stationary state.

Far more than physical energy enters into the production of high-quality goods and services. It is impossible to reduce the work involved in the writing of James Joyce's *Ulysses* or the development of quantum theory to their equivalence in fossil-fuel units of energy. If such an equivalence existed, we would be helpless to explain the phenomena of classical Athens, Elizabethan England, or Renaissance Italy. After all the entire consumption of physical energy in such societies was negligible by our standards.

The fallacy of the Odums is that they treat our economico-ecological complex as though it were a homogeneous system, when it is in fact composed of several subsystems each with its specific logic. They attempt to assimilate everything into the ecological-resources subsystem, just as conventional economists try imposing the logic of the pure and perfect market on the other subsystems. The great contribution of the Odums is to have mapped the circuits of the energy subsystem of our economy. There is no way in which the economy can go on functioning unless that subsystem is in balance. Though a subsystem, it is an all-pervasive one. It has an undisputed primacy in the hierarchy of subsystems. Whatever the laws of society, they are subject to the laws of physics. And yet, within the matrix of energy constraints, other purely social laws of a very distinct sort operate. They are not to be confused with physical laws; their codes are different. What is more, they generate powerful feedbacks into the energy subsystem, that can assure or disrupt its smooth functioning.

If we add to the subsystems already described the Ecological and Non-Renewable Resources Subsystem we arrive at the following model:

The Ecological Subsystem will send important information to the economy through price changes. The exhaustion of inexpensive sources of non-renewable resources will feed a negative input into price – i.e. the smaller the amount of available resources, the higher their prices will tend to become. Such higher prices for depleted resources will stimulate further exploration, research and development in the field: the complete causal loop thus traced between the Ecological System and Price will tend to be self-equilibrating. However, if governments misread the price signals from the Ecological Subsystem and try suppressing the higher prices triggered by occurrences in it, this self-balancing mechanism is destroyed. That is a good way to ensure a major disaster ahead.

Not all price increases will have this balancing effect on the availability of non-renewable resources. Higher interest rates and increased costs for the labor and materials that enter into the exploitation and development of new sources of the depleted materials will have a negative effect on their supply: they will tend to make infeasible projects in the area that were economic at previous cost levels.

Though complex, the above model is less complex than reality itself. It is necessary to keep track of that reality and to ensure that our theorizing does not fly in the face of it. 'Any system that cannot be modeled cannot be managed'.[10]

There are in fact other important subsystems that I have not

10 Hazel Henderson, *The Entropy State,* Planning Review, April, May, 1974. Another school of thought on this subject commands a far greater following among economists. Thus Milton Friedman writes: "On the other side, the quantity theorist must sharply limit, and be prepared to specify explicitly, the variables that it is empirically important to include in the function. For to expand the number of variables regarded as significant is to empty the hypothesis of its empirical content; there is indeed little if any difference

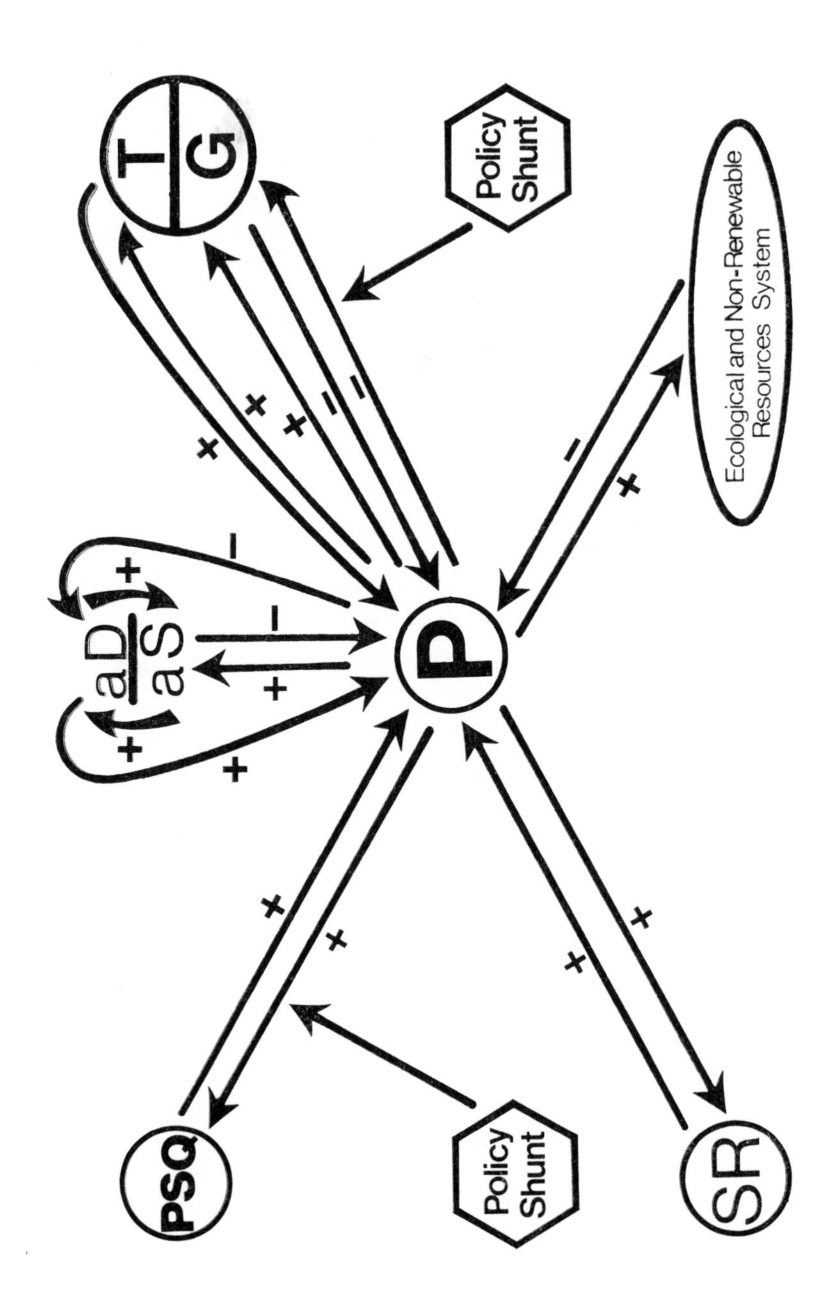
T
G
Policy Shunt
Ecological and Non-Renewable Resources System
aD
aS
P
PSQ
Policy Shunt
SR

included in our chart. Whenever a distinct logic takes over and sets the patterns of economic behavior, a subsystem takes form. Thus there is a demographic subsystem that follows laws and rhythms quite its own, and feeds decisive influences into the other subsystems and, of course, receives input from them.

One such subsystem, of course, may preempt our attention, and lead us to neglect another that in the final analysis and in the longer time perspective may be vastly more important. Moreover, few analyses are really that 'final'. That is why even penetrating analyses of our problems may suffer less from basic error than from a foreshortening of perspective. This does not necessarily invalidate them for specific purposes; it merely makes them inadequate to encompass our full problem.[11]

The purpose of our overall chart is to remind us that our economy is made up of distinct subsystems, each with its peculiar logic; and that the whole is imbedded in any environment of objective constraints.[12] All these subsystems debouch into price. This being so, price cannot be understood in terms of any single monistic theory – whether marginal utility, the labor theory of value, or any other. It is the resultant of

---

between asserting that the demand for money is highly unstable and asserting that it is a perfectly stable function of an indefinitely large number of variables.' *(The Quantity Theory of Money – A Restatement of Monetary Theory and Policy – Major contributions to Contemporary Thought* – Edited by Richard S. Thorn, Random House, N.Y., 1966, p. 80). We have here a perfect instance of tailoring the client to the cloth.

11 A good example of this is the excellent work of Robert Bacon and Walter Eltis, *Britain's Economic Problem: Too Few Producers,* London, 1976, The Macmillan Press Ltd. The book adopts a point of view that in some respects is similar to the one I develop. The focus, however, is on 'how Britain went wrong,' rather than on how economic theory went wrong and contributed so richly to Britain's troubles.

12 'The multi-level phenomena of social life and especially the hierarchy of administration, control and bureaucry have engaged the attention of a whole series of sociologists since the time of Max Weber.

'It is surprising that economists should have neglected for so long the problem of multi-level phenomena, especially given the analogies provided by other branches of science.' Janos Kornai, *Anti-Equilibrium. On Economic Systems Theory and Tasks of Research,* North-Holland Publishing Company, Amsterdam, London, 1971, p. 84. From a study of economic administration and decision-making on either side of the Iron Curtain, Kornai develops a powerful critique of conventional economic theory from the systems viewpoint. The systems that he is primarily concerned with are those within the firm and planning apparatus. My goal is a broader one: to describe and trace the circuitry of the different economic subsystems within society at large.

superimposed rationales, and its structure must therefore be additive – we must add up components of cost, rather than deduce the result in advance from the *a priori* concepts of any one theory. In a pluralistic economy price is something to be unscrambled and decoded, like the complex messages that come over our telephone lines. We must dismiss no part of that message as mere noise, because it does not conform to the pattern prescribed by our Subsystem One. Price, for example, may be signalling to us the imminent exhaustion of our energy resources, or the pressure of population upon food supplies. If we ignore this and try to force price into preconceived patterns, we are in fact slaying the messenger bringing us the bad news.

Most of the blunders committed by economists result from the misapplication of the logic of one system to something taking place in another system. Whenever an activity is transferred from one subsystem to another, an *intersectorial transformation* occurs. There are definite transform functions connected with such transfers. Thus the classic of freshman courses – the GNP goes down whenever a man marries his housekeeper – is a simple instance of such an intersectorial transform. I have not included the intrahousehold subsystem in our chart because it does not affect price, but it does exist. And when a man marries his housekeeper, her functions are transferred from the market to the intra-household subsystem. And hence the GNP goes down.

The fallacy of composition uncovered by Keynes is another such instance. Balancing the budget of an individual or a firm is provident policy; from that it does not follow that it is equally wise for a government to balance its budget during a depression. Not even golden rules can be moved from a market microeconomic system to a macroeconomic system without undergoing a transformation.

In recent years our price policy has been studded with like errors arising from the neglect of the necessary intersectorial transforms. Thus when the public sector grows significantly as part of the economy, it does not matter that aggregate supply and demand balance: price cannot remain stable because part of the activity has shifted from the private to the public sector; the necessary transform affects price via the social lien. Likewise, you cannot force prices to stay flat under such circumstances by restricting money supply or raising interest rates. These measures are directed to the market sector, while the price movement originates in the Social Lien Subsystem, or the Social Revalorization Subsystem. We would be attempting to influence happenings in one subsystem by applying the logic of another.

Chapter Four

Entropy – Fine-Tuning for the Heat Death

The subsystems of our economy have each its own logic; but these logics do interact. The common denominator for this interaction is to be found in the entropy concept. Only by learning to reason in entropy terms will we be able to manage our mixed economy.

Early in the 19th century a French engineer, Sadi Carnot, pondered a fact familiar to every housewife: heat flows only from a hotter to a colder body. In time this led to the science of thermodynamics. Its second law – the entropy law – tells us that energy is available for use only if a difference in energy levels exists. Though simple enough, the idea stood Newtonian physics on its ear. Up to then its laws had been taken to be as valid read backward as read forward. But once the notion was introduced of potential differences running out, of the so-called 'heat death', time became as unidirectional as the rest of us. Nature acquired a history and a shadow.

Entropy – the running out of negentropy – bids well to become the dominant symbolism of our day. It is coming to pervade every area of social thinking with but a single exception – economic theory. Walras's equations set up a non-entropic model: they are self-equilibrating. In this model there is simply nothing to run out – unless it is our credulity.

Nicholas Georgescu-Roegen has touched upon this prodigy: 'But by the time Jevons and Walras began laying the cornerstones of modern economics, a spectacular revolution in physics had already brought the downfall of the mechanistic dogma both in the natural sciences and in philosophy. And the curious fact is that none of the architects of "the mechanics of utility and self-interest" and even none of the latter-day model builders seems to have been aware at any time of this downfall.' [1]

Our reasoning on economic subjects is thus imprisoned in a non-

1 *The Entropy Law and the Economic Process,* Harvard University Press, Cambridge, 1971, p. 2.

entropy model. And what is worse, this model, promising the music of the spheres, has been incongruously wedded to the Keynesian model that is the living embodiment of exponential growth. We are thus faced with the task of expressing the needs of an entropy-menaced society in terms of a model whose exponential structure is masked by equilibrium dogma. This contradiction underlies the sorry performance of economic theory over the past decade.

To remedy this we must begin by extending the entropy concept from a purely physical one to take in analogous social phenomena. For all his brilliant scholarship, Georgescu-Roegen is concerned exclusively with physical entropy as it affects economics. Hazel Henderson, indeed, has given the entropy notion a directly social connotation. Her *Entropy State* portrays dramatically the gathering entropy of our society.[2]

---

2 *Planning Review*, April-May, 1974. At every term we are confronted with writers who prove helpless to handle the problems of our environmental entropies with the tools provided by our non-entropic economic theory. Thus in his recent *The Poverty of Power – Energy and the Economic Crisis* (Alfred A. Knopf, New York, 1976, pp. 64 and 80) Barry Commoner sounds some apocalyptic alarms. And yet he does not take us far when he comes to economic analysis. He leads up to something like a punch-line when he charges the oil companies with depending increasingly on imports, and with seeming more interested in making money than in proving up domestic reserves. I should have thought that under a market system that could safely be taken for granted. With interest rates mounting as a result of our structural price gradient, proving up oil reserves too far in advance could become a form of corporative suicide.

On the American synthetic oil program Commoner remarks: 'Now Mr. Ford has discovered how to make up for the inability of the private companies to assume these risks. He is offering them public funds. . . . But the new scheme has a special kind of irony. It proposes to use public funds to guarantee an enterprise that would burden the people in the United States with higher fuel prices if it succeeds or with higher taxes if it fails.'

I have no idea whether the Ford scheme was excessively generous to the private companies. But what emerges clearly is the inability of the author to think out physical depletion problems in terms of economic entropies. Once he leaves the purely material aspects of the problem he takes refuge in old-fashioned radical rhetoric like a floundering swimmer who finally makes it to dry land. Thus, are higher fuel prices necessarily proof of a 'rip-off'? May they not reflect that higher risks and costs and be needed to curtail consumption? And if private corporations are unable to assume the gamble of bringing synthetic oil onto the market without public underwriting, are we to conclude that the state should take over the entire project? Perhaps it should. But all that would have to be thought out in terms of the new entropy patterns around us, including the entropy of economic bureaucracy.

It omits a key aspect, however: the possibility of identifying and tapping quite new negentropies to extend our entropy system and revitalize our society. It is true that our problems do threaten to prove of a terminal character, but they are not inevitably so. I shall return to Hazel Henderson and this matter.

Implicitly in most discussions of entropy as it affects society, the notion of social entropy has already crept in. It is rarely an exclusively physical entropy that we are talking about. Thus when we refer to the entropy of fuel consumption, we hardly mean that the temperature of the world has risen so much as a result of our fuel combustion that the differentials no longer exist to allow heat to flow. Nor is it even that we are running out of fuel deposits. These exist; but those that lend themselves to economic exploitation are being depleted. However, the notion of accessibility and economic feasibility are complex and only in part relate to the physical nature of the deposits. Of equal importance will be the technology of transportation, location, labor costs, interest rates, taxation, conservationist restrictions, and other factors that have little relevance to a strictly physical notion of entropy. Increased fuel consumption gives rise to social and material conditions that interfere with the utilization of what non-renewable fuel reserves still remain. The entropy that concerns us is really a hybrid of material and social factors.

Physicists have provided a useful bridge to help us carry the entropy concept from the purely physical to the social realm. Statistical thermodynamics views entropy as a degradation from order to disorder, a reshuffling and a levelling of discrete states. This idea can be applied not only to energy states, but to physical stocks. Thus when we consume a metal item, we do not destroy it. Just as in the mining and refining of metals we concentrate them, so, too, in using up we scatter them by such processes as rusting (chemical)and erosion (physical). They are still there, but to reenter the productive cycle they would have to be reconcentrated. Statistical thermodynamics, indeed, attempts to reduce differences of potential level to the distribution of molecules and energy amongst the theoretically possible states.[3]

---

3 See Georgescu-Roegen, op. cit. pp. 7 et seq. for a discussion of the attempt of Boltzmann and others to equate entropy with thermodynamic probability and thus bring back the reversibility of Newtonian mechanics. The tug to symmetrical models is powerfully rooted in the human mind; Lord Kelvin related this to the fact that it is only by reversible motion that man is able to act on his environment.

This insight can be transferred directly to the socio-economic sphere. Thus the difference between a rigorously hierarchized society and a pluralistic one will relate to the distribution of levels of education and political and economic power, as well as to their permanence and the gaps amongst them. The export prosperity of Britain throughout most of the 19th century was due in part to the one-sided distribution of industry in the world. And so forth.

In thermodynamics entropy is expressed by the formula $\int dQ/T$, where dQ is the heat flow and T the absolute temperature. When we transfer this formula to economico-social phenomena, T will not always be the stock of the same item of which dQ is the flow. In essence the task is the following: not only to trace the dwindling of a certain stock, but to take cognizance of the diminishing functional value of the residual stock because of the declining difference in potential.[4]

We can define economic negentropy as the potential difference needed to assure the means and motivations for the functioning of a subsystem. That such a definition covers a wide range of phenomena does not detract from its aptness. On the contrary, it strengthen its correspondence with the thermodynamic prototype. In physics differences of energy levels can take on many forms – chemical, thermal, nuclear, hydraulic, electromagnetic, gravitational, and so forth. Any of these may be tapped to reverse the energy flow in another entropy system. An entropy system may thus be enlarged, but never really reversed. Viewed as a unit, the systems joined run down, not up. There is no way of bootlegging negentropy.

An example of two entropy systems interacting can be found in the case of the social mobility of the advanced countries and the consumption of fossil fuels. As the reshuffling of social orders proceeded with the development of our pluralistic society, manual labor became both expensive and in short supply. More reliance therefore came to be put on energy consumption. The children of manual workers, re-

4 A formula could be set up as follows. Let R = the remaining stock; T = the lower potential level in the entropy system. What we are seeking then is F (the functional value) of the remaining stock:

$$F = (R-dR) . \frac{R-dR/T+dR}{R/T}$$

In that equation I am assuming a linear relationship connecting the function with the potential differential. A more general formula would be:

$$F = (R-dR) . \frac{\varnothing(R-dR)/T+dR)}{\varnothing(R/T)}$$

flecting the heightened social mobility, became white-collar workers and professionals, thus increasing the demand for other people's manual services even as the supply of such labor declined. Housewives turned their backs on domestic drudgery and took to packaged, pre-cooked foods, and electrical appliances. Even tooth-brushes came to be electrified. All this, however, sped another entropy accumulation – that of non-renewable fossil-fuels. In this instance a social entropy system drew upon the negentropy of a physical system.

The history of industrial society could be retold in terms of entropy systems. As entropy built up in one area, new negentropy sources were found and piped in. The pressure of the growing industrial population on food supplies that so concerned Ricardo after the Napoleonic Wars was overcome through the abolition of the Corn Laws, and by the opening up of the pampas of the New World by revolutions in land and ocean transport. The need for ever expanding markets felt by the industrial system that resulted was met by an aggressive colonialism and the export of capital. The crisis of the 1930's due to the lack of effective demand was resolved by the Keynesian revolution. Keynesian techniques in turn contributed to the expansion of the public sector to the point where it has come to adulterate the price signals and ethic of the market. The private sector is simply running out of elbowroom. That is where we find ourselves today. It is not necessarily the end of the world; but it does mean that we shall have to seek out some major, new negentropy sources.

Once we recognize this underlying pattern, new negentropy sources will not be hard to find. Multiple, accelerating change is the hallmark of our times, and this gives rise to new game rules, to new potential dfferences. Similarly every geological upheaval threw up a new topography of rivers, lakes and waterfalls. With the proper theory, it will be possible to survey and harness these new sources of negentropy to reverse the build-up of social and even material entropies.

Some theories have captured one aspect or another of the entropic structure of the economy.

Ricardo's system was an entropic one: food became dearer as less productive lands were brought under cultivation to feed the industrial towns; as money wages rose to cover these costs, profit, as the residue, declined.

Marx's system was entropic. The increasing portion of 'constant' capital (non-labor investment) due to technological change led to a falling rate of profit; for in this system surplus value arises only from the 'variable capital' invested in labor-power. To counter this, the capitalists were driven to expand their operations. Inevitably they ran out of vital space.

Like all entropic theories of the past, Marx's, too, concentrated upon a single entropy. Its focus was on the difference between labor's productivity in industry and that in pre-capitalist societies; for it was the latter that in large measure determined the wages that the employers paid their workers. Capitalism drew its principal negentropy from this potential difference.

Marx was, to be sure, aware of other negentropies: he credited the capitalist with a sharp nose for gain wherever an opportunity might present itself – new technology, organizational changes, in a ranging quest for markets. But to all these he assigned a secondary importance – they served to make possible the creation and realization of surplus value on an ever greater scale. The purpose of this was seen in the appropriation of the unpaid portion of labor's production. The capitalist's other contributions were viewed merely as hastening the historic doom of the unsuspecting fool. There was no suggestion that these other talents of the capitalist (with exception of his gift for technical innovation) might be needed under socialism. In keeping with this bias, Marx considered the entire field of distribution as unproductive.

Useful as such a model may have been for the understanding of 19th-century capitalism, it is hardly helpful today. Nevertheless it continues to shape the thinking not only of Marxists, but of many non-political trade unionists. No matter what a firm may be paying its workers, no matter that it may be losing money, by definition it is still exploiting them, though it may not be able to 'realize' its surplus value due to the 'inherent contradictions of capitalism.'

And yet labor's wages in the advanced countries are set less by the employers, or even by the market, than by institutional factors: governments and unions. So much so that John K. Galbraith has formulated his popular indictment of large corporations for conniving with 'Big Labor' in *not* resisting demands for higher wages, but instead passing such increased costs on to the consumer.

In the light of entropy theory that charge could be reformulated as an analysis: capitalists no longer see as their prime negentropy source the gap between labor's productivity and labor's wages. For their profits they have come to depend upon quite other negentropies, including those of market strategies. The last-century view of private enterprise as first and last an exploiter of labor turns out to have been a historically determined special case of a more general law. Entrepreneurs must be recognized as negentropy scouts with a special gift for tracking down and harnessing negentropy sources. .Much of the economic grief of our world – on either side of the Iron Curtain – stems from the failure to recognize the broader counter-entropic role of private enterprise.

A distinction must be drawn between micro- and macro-negentropy. Macro-negentropy would refer to a completely new negentropy horizon, the identification of a new type of negentropy or the discovery of major quantities of a familiar negentropy. Micro-negentropy, on the other hand, would denote a limited local source of potential difference – the market scarcity of a particular commodity, an improvement in organization, technique, or distribution.

In its day-to-day functions the state has little enough to do with the development of new negentropy sources. Bureaucracy is a great leveller of differences into averages; in a pluralistic society, moreover, it is a goal of government to iron out the grosser inequalities. And where ideology leaves off, the sheer metabolism of the state takes over – it gnaws at whatever bone is not yet bare, and in doing so further reduces potential differences.

Under special circumstances, however, the state can become a mighty purveyor of macro-negentropy. At turning points of history, in the hands of charismatic leaders, it may open up macro-negentropies that the entrepreneur alone would be helpless to unseal. For it falls to the state to change the game rules. A classic example of this was Roosevelt in the thirties. Wars and drastic tariff changes can also be productive of macro-negentropies. On the other hand, the economy is dependent upon private enterprise for almost all of its micro-negentropy.

Entropy problems are by no means confined to our side of the Iron Curtain. Although at certain times and in certain areas, Communist lands may be rich in macro-negentropy, they are woefully deficient in micro-negentropy. Without an adequate market, response to consumer needs is difficult at best. That is why we find the provisioning of Moscow and Leningrad in fruits and vegetables ludicrously dependent upon Georgian and Armenian traders flying on passenger planes with suitcases full of such items. In some respects distribution has been thrown back to Marco Polo's day when the merchant accompanied his wares. The legalization of free peasant markets – first under Lenin's New Economic Policy and again more recently – was an admission of the incompetence of the state to tap micro-negentropy.

Basically both the Communist and Western worlds suffer each

from its 'theory-trap' that incapacitates it to deal adequately with its entropy build-up. The outcome of their rivalry is likely to be decided as much by which side will manage to free itself from its theory-trap as by their stockpiles of nuclear weapons.

Let me review some of the entropy systems in our economy.

1. *Depletion of the reserves of manual labor resulting from an upward social mobility.*

The dramatic broadening of educational opportunities, the decay of the apprentice system, and the social revalorization characteristic of a pluralistic society have had drastic effects on the cost, the quality, and availability of manual labor. At the same time the entry of many of the children of manual laborers into the middle class has increased the demand for manual services.

To cope with this entropy, other entropy systems have been drawn upon. A good example is the common practice in the advanced countries of discarding entire sub-assemblies of automobiles and appliances to avoid making minor repairs. Entire automobiles, indeed, are scrapped that in the underveloped countries would be kept running for further decades. This transfers some of the entropy build-up from the manual labor system to that of energy and non-renewable resources.

Another means of dealing with this entropy has been the liberalization of immigration laws. In this way the developed lands acquire recruits who are prepared to do the hard, dirty, menial work that natives are increasingly shying away from. In effect we are tapping the vast potential difference between the social and economic conditions in various parts of the world. Like all negentropy transfusions, this one, too, involves an eventual entropy build-up of its own. Inevitably the offspring of the immigrants – and often the immigrants themselves – become assimilated to local standards and add to the magnitude of the original problem.

There are ways in which such secondary entropy build-up is restrained. These are not consciously planned by the host lands, but for all that they are hardly less important for their economies. The most notable is illegal immigration. Entire industries in the United States and Canada could not operate without the vast influx of illegal immigrants from Latin America and the Caribbean countries. In this demographic pressures and the gaps in economic potential assert themselves with an elemental force. The illegal status of such immigrants segregates them and rules out their assimilation to local standards. They have little access to social insurance, and often keep their children out of the schools. What deportations occur serve to dramatize the segregated status of the illegal workers, rather than to do away with the phenomenon.

The granting of work permits to immigrants for limited periods is a more formal technique for achieving the same end.

2. *Consumers' Entropy* is closely associated with the foregoing.

Much of the progress of capitalism was related to the improved living that resulted as consumers came to satisfy more of their needs on the market. So long as they were able to draw on the labor of marginal workers, while their own income reflected their role in an industrial economy, Consumers' Negentropy was available to them. They benefited from the gulf in economic status that separated them from the workers serving their needs. In this way the middle class freed itself from much domestic drudgery by drawing upon rural and immigrant help, by buying processed and prepackaged foods; they travelled to countries where prices were at a lower level, and so forth.

In an increasingly pluralistic world Consumers' Negentropy is rapidly giving out. Legislation has lessened the difference in earnings of manual workers and professionals. Then, too, there is the dwindling importance of mass-produced commodities in our economy as contrasted with services: for it is only mass-produced goods that can absorb steeply higher wages without sharp increases of their end price. And there is, too, the injection of increasing amounts of taxation into each market transaction. When our chores are done for us by others, not only are we taking in each other's washing at wages that are increasingly similar, but the state takes a growing bite every time the laundry bundles change hands.

An equation for Consumers' Entropy can be set up as follows. Let LRI (Labor Replacement Index) express the ratio of the cost of the substitute marketed labor drawn upon to the rate of the consumer's own earnings. Let SL (Social Lien) represent the proportion of taxation shifting into the price of the replacement goods or services to their entire price. When the product $(1 + SL) \times LRI$ approaches unity, the build-up of Consumers' Entropy has begun. (To complete the picture, of course, there should be an adjustment for the shift in the relative importance of mass-produced commodities in consumers' purchases as explained above).

As this build-up proceeds, a point will be reached where the purchaser's living standard will actually decline every time he goes to the market to replace a service that he has been performing for himself. And his living standard would benefit if he were to reverse the trend and become less dependent upon the market. That is the basis of the 'do-it-yourself' trend that is coming to the fore.

Many of the budgetary straits of the citizen today, though too readily blamed upon exploitation, are in fact related to this build-up of Consumers' Entropy. No labor leader can rise above the role of demagogue unless he has acquired and passed on to his followers some perception of this factor.

Consumers' Entropy involves an intersectorial transform. A service is shifted from the intrahousehold sector to the market sector. The value taken on by the transform will vary with the difference between the consumer's own earning potential and that of the person whose services he acquires, as well as with the amount of social lien entering into the transaction.

3. Of crucial importance today is the entropy associated with *the dwindling vital space left to the private sector within the economy.*

Elsewhere I have classified the different categories of state services according to their influence upon price and the economy.[5] That analysis is critically related to the whole subject of entropy. Traditional state functions such as courts, police, prisons, armies, tax-collectors, I termed *core state functions.* Another type of state function I called *paraproductive* – these are not unlike those provided by the private sector and contribute directly to improved living standards. Examples of the latter would be highways, schools, health services. To the traditional core state services we would be well advised to assimilate those connected with economic policing and controls.

There is, to begin with, a distinct entropy accumulation resulting from the growing proportion of the national income going to the state – no matter whether it is spent on core services or paraproductive ones. With the prodigious growth of the public sector, the setting in which private enterprise must work changes beyond recognition. Because of the enormous increase of the social lien component in price, as well as other components originating in non-market subsystems, the price signals of the market become addled and its negentropy undermined.

Within the public sector itself, however, a parallel entropy build-up takes place. The greater the portion of the public budget devoted to core state functions, the less the resources that remain for paraproductive purposes. And whereas paraproductive services are likely to contribute to the health and productivity of society, core state services can

5 Krehm. p. 82.

have, at times, quite the contrary effect.

It is ever easier to behold the mote in one's neighbor's eye than the beam in one's own. Let us therefore apply this analysis to the distribution problems of the U.S.S.R. As the sixth decade of the revolution draws to its close the Soviets have brought core state services to a phenomenal flower. To its concentration camps, secret police, censorship, to the vigilant ladies who grace every floor of every hotel noting who comes and who goes, Moscow has added the world's largest navy. And much else. All these items come under the heading of core state services.

On the other hand the U.S.S.R. remains picturesquely underprovided with the most elementary services that we take for granted – filling stations and repair facilities for its expanding fleet of private cars, retail outlets, restaurants, and so forth.

It might seem a simple enough matter for the homeland of Sputnik to make such things available. And yet that could prove an illusion. With so staggering a proportion of the national effort taken up with core state functions, the resources are not readily at hand to expand such paraproductive services. And these, of course, must take care of vast areas that fall to the private sector in the West. On top of that, there is the lack of scope for entrepreneurial talent to seek out the micro-negentropies to do such a job well.

In the Western world we are witnessing a somewhat parallel trend. We are rapidly building up a core-state entropy of our own: an expanding economic bureaucracy leans heavily upon administrative fiat to control an economy that it has taken few pains to understand. It is abetted in this by the failure of economic theory. Having advanced the unrealisable expectation of stable price in a mixed economy, that theory has necessarily abdicated any further serious intervention in policy-making. Instead that is left to hard-knuckled administrators who have a naive faith that economic problems can be resolved by citing subsections of articles of bureaucratic gobbledegook. Increasingly our economic decisions are being made by non-economic logic.

This has a double cost, each component of which has been ignored. The sheer bulk of this bureaucracy adds to the dead weight of taxation in price. And since that officialdom breathes the very spirit of arbitrary routine, it blocks the seeking out of new negentropy sources upon which the survival of our society depends. Salvation instead is sought by trying to force prices back to equilibrium points which in fact do not exist.[6]

4. *The negentropy of reserves.*

Due to the very unpredicability of the market, an excess of production and distribution facilities come into being. In the Marxist view this was always deemed wasteful, and to an extent it is. Yet dismissing it as *merely* wasteful belongs to a lost age of innocence when socialism was an immaculate utopia rather than a dusty, sexagenarian experience. And the length of the queues in the U.S.S.R. should warn us that there is another aspect to the over-supply of facilities that the free market throws up. They can in fact be likened to the parallel circuits employed in cybernetics to provide a higher degree of reliability – insurance against the failure or the overcrowding of a single circuit in series. Such reliability circuits in cybernetics were, in turn, inspired by reliability systems in biology.[7]

A free market creates such reserve circuits automatically. An excess of them leads to loss for the entrepreneur or even outright ruin.

---

6 Italy's spreading underground phenomenon of *lavoro nero* offers an example of new negentropy sources ferreted out by private enterprise to salvage what might seem beyond redemption. *Time* (August 22nd, 1977) reports: 'With wage gains quickly eroded by runaway inflation . . . nearly 5 million "unemployed, retired and sick" people – a fifth of the nation's total labor force – work full or part time at jobs that do not officially exist. Another 3 million are believed to moonlight regularly at unreported second and even third jobs. Entire families work at home assembling ball-point pens, making shoes, stamping out auto parts or upholstering furniture . . . cops and firemen do lucrative plumbing and electrical work in their spare time. Many are substandard . . . but there are no tax or social security deductions. . . . Companies lease sophisticated and expensive machinery and make direct loans to help families set up cellar factories whose workers labor all hours to meet delivery dates. Even the biggest Italian . . . subsidiaries may buy components from suppliers who use black labor. . . . The government has so far not acted on pleas from clothing manufacturers that it cancel a contract for 70,000 carabinieri uniforms awarded to two small companies that underbid competitors by 50%, presumably by turning to cellar or cottage workshops. . . ."

Clearly there are socially undesirable aspects to such an arrangement. A better appreciation of economic entropy by governments would make it unnecessary for private enterprise to go underground to open up new negentropy sources.

7 Oskar Lange *Introduction to Economic Cybernetics,* translated from the Polish by Jozef Stadler, Pergamon Press, Oxford and Warsaw, 1970, p. 165: 'In an individual organism a great number of reserve elements gives it a high degree of reliability of survival and activity. . . . We can see with one eye, breathe with one lung, live with one kidney or one brain lobe. The second eye, lung, kidney, or brain lobe are reserve elements.'

He is prepared to brave that risk because of the lure of greater than normal profits if he guesses correctly. Nobody can induce him to create such socially useful reserves without the prospect of such rewards. Policy directed at suppressing the rewards without removing the risks must end up by depriving society of these reliability reserves.

Most politically-inspired price controls have been devoted to just such near-sighted objectives. Thus in the housing industry an over-built situation is not unusual on the free market. When this happens, apartments will be rented at below break-even rents, and homes will be sold at a loss for those who built them. Such periods of overbuilding, however, alternate with periods of relative under-supply when rents and house prices catch up with and even surpass costs and normal profits. If governments take the rents established during the gluts as the norm and attempt to adjust the rents of the scarcity periods to them, the result is not hard to foresee. There will be no motivation to create 'reliability reserves', or for that matter even to catch up with the backlog of housing needs.

The penalty for not respecting the negentropy of this system is clear in the Communist countries. Translated from the symbolism of cybernetics to human terms, the absence of 'reliability circuits' in the U.S.S.R. means billions of man-hours spent in the boredom of the triple-queuing that goes on in retail outlets – one queue for the purchase, one for payment at the cashier's wicket, and the final one for picking up the parcel. Add to this the time that goes to tracking down scarce consumers's goods, the crush to get at merchandise that is above shoddy quality, the impaired quality of life under these conditions. Parallel distribution circuits for greater 'reliability' can play as important a role in the economy of a nation as additional steel plants. Indeed, they are not without their effect on steel production.

Trends inherent in our mixed economy in themselves tend to deplete this 'negentropy of reserves'. Higher labor costs, taxation, interest rates have all raised the penalty for carrying excessive inventories of housing, merchandise, or for building excess industrial plant. That makes it all the more necessary to attune public policy – *especially* where this takes the form of controls – to the delicate logic of this negentropy.

5. *Interest rate entropy.*

A key potential difference is that created by the spread between interest rates and the entrepreneur's prospective rate of profit. Wicksell and the earlier Keynes based much of their reasoning on this factor; but they saw it essentially as a cyclical affair. This the structural price gradient in our mixed economy has changed. The price ramp is discounted by money-lenders and translated into an interest-rate gradient. And this is happening at a time when the uncertainties arising from the transformations of our economy surround the entrepreneurial function with a heightened degree of risk. The margin has thus narrowed between lenders' interest rates and foreseeable entrepreneurial profits appropriately discounted for risk.

The distribution pattern between rentier and entrepreneur has thus become unsettled – to the disadvantage of the latter.

And yet society stands in need of the contribution of the entrepreneur as rarely in the past. The very scope of our social restructurings calls for even more sweeping changes ahead. These will be of a far more complex nature than would appear from the popular stricture: 'We must learn to live within our means.' For 'we', 'means', and our concept of 'live' have all changed beyond recognition during the past generation. Not only has the world experienced a population explosion of shattering dimension, but the aspirations of entire classes, nations and continents have been lifted out of their secular grooves. A dynamic remaking of traditional relationships is irrevocably under way; we must learn to direct it within the constraints imposed by our resources. That will call for capital expenditures on an unprecedented scale.

Given this vista, our interest-rate entropy can have grave implications. For example, despite our growing fuel famine, even the harnessing of remaining hydro-electric sites can be made infeasible if interest rates move too high. That is still more the case of projects on technological frontiers where a great element of gamble exists.

In one of its aspects, the price system may be seen as the economy's antennae, alert to early warnings from the market of necessary change. But on basic, long-term matters the response of the economy to what price is signalling will depend to a significant degree on interest rates. To complicate matters further, the long-term interest rate is a function of long-term price expectations. We thus have a disturbing positive feedback from price to long-term interest rates. That is tantamount to saying that there is a *negative* feedback from our warning signal to the sensitivity of our response to it.[8]

---

8 How delicate the balance of decision, and how serious the inadequacy of the response to price signals appears from the following passage of Philip Connelly and Robert Perlman *(The Policies of Scarcity – Resource conflicts in International Relations,* Oxford University Press, London, New York and Toronto,

6. *The Keynesian entropy.*

The very depth of the economic crisis of the thirties provided a relatively simple cure for it. Along with employment, prices, too, had fallen precipitously; the role of the public sector in the economy was still modest. Though the automatic forces of the market were helpless to correct the situation, the means for doing so were plentifully at hand. Once the economists and the governments had restructured their thinking, powerful new negentropies could be tapped to achieve the desired result.

Most of these negentropies have since given out. The public sector has grown to such proportions that it interferes seriously with the functioning of private enterprise. Were there a realization of the negentropies that must be respected to keep private enterprise operative, it would still be possible to accommodate even so large a public sector in a mixed economy. Policy, however, is set by a weird combination of the theory of a century ago and the short-term requirements of the political arena. Under these circumstances the private sector threatens to grind to a halt.

At the time of this writing, the point is illustrated by the faltering efforts of the Western countries to drag themselves out of a recession that to a large extent was government-induced. At present the exercise is in its third year with very unconvincing results.

Within the scenario of stable prices, there is no way left in which governments can intervene with the classical Keynesian therapy. That was conceived for a cyclical depression; government spending was meant to help both prices and economic activity recover for the depths. At present, though governments have directed their deflationary fire at bringing prices into line, the price gradient is one of the few things that

---

1975) 'Since October, 1973, however, oil has ceased to seem so cheap, even if it remains competitive with a range of other energy sources. In theory, that change should have helped to bring home the potential shortage of oil and encourage precautionary action. . . . In practice, the very fact that energy costs constitute such a small proportion of average final production costs makes it more difficult for the price mechanism to work effectively in providing such an adjustment to a scarcity of oil. In such circumstances, when the commodity in short supply has little effect on final prices, cost increases can more easily be passed onto customers or absorbed in other ways. Price effects alone may then not result in a rapid enough reaction to the growing shortage, and the crisis may be sharpened by being delayed. . . .'

Add a needlessly high interest rate to this picture and the result may be a disastrously sluggish response to critical prices messages.

the deflationary operation has left intact. Any increase in government spending therefore can only add further to the social lien in price and cause prices to move up even faster. Or if as a result of the intervention the private sector does recover and thus expand the tax base to reduce the burden of social lien per unit output, profit margins will have to be allowed to recover. And in many instances that, too, can only mean higher prices.

The usual recourse of governments to encouraging house sales and other 'big ticket' items as a countercyclical measure is no longer available. Every entropy build-up described in this chapter has contributed to pushing up housing costs. These have risen to a point where most housing at the moment is beyond the means of a great part of the population. Only the prospect of increased wages and other earnings could revive the housing market. That, however, would mean a continuation of the price gradient. Our whole economy in fact depends for its functioning on the negentropies arising from the price gradient that our governments have been trying to suppress or ignore.

The Keynesian therapy has succumbed to its own peculiar entropy build-up. That is why our present recession was so much easier for governments to bring about than to cure.

This is a special case of:

7. *The entropy of theory.*

At best, any economic theory focusses its attention on a single favored entropy system. Its validity will thus depend upon that particular negentropy not having run out. But by their very nature negentropies do wind down, while theories have a way of perduring. It is from this discrepancy that many of society's troubles flow.

Under classical capitalism the primary negentropy that served the entrepreneur was the gap between the productivity of the industrial economy and the living standard of the workers. This greatly eased the task of those who challenged the status quo.

It was not necessary to think out too carefully where the resources would come from to improve the lot of the underprivileged. So glaring were the inequalities of distribution, that closer accountancy could safely be left to the capitalists.[9]

9 Thus George R. Feiwell sums up Michal Kalecki's thought as follows: 'Kalecki distinguished three major ways of generating effective demand in a modern capitalist economy and reflected upon their adequacy and relative efficiency in effecting and supporting full employment. He concentrated on the relative merits of (1) deficit spending, (2) stimulating private investment and (3)

That constituted a valuable negentropy for theorists, but it is a negentropy that has become seriously impaired. It is no longer possible to assume the existence of ample reserves in the capitalists' coffers that can be drawn on to satisfy politically expedient programs. When governments make such an assumption – and they too often do – they may find themselves cutting into living tissue of the private sector that is necessary for its survival. Nor when this occurs, is it enough to improvise some 'incentive' to get the private sector operating in the given area once more. Respecting the negentropy of the private sector is by no means the same as bribing or subsidizing it. Negentropy depends not upon a certain amount of money changing hands, but on the functional feasibility of a circuit.

The resources to pay the subsidy, for example, will often be raised by the state through taxation that will load the price structure with social lien and put some goods and services (including at times those that are being subsidized) beyond the reach of the social group for whom they are intended. I shall return to this matter.

When the private sector is reduced to dependence upon subsidies, it forfeits some of its capability as negentropy scout; it becomes annexed to the logic of the public sector. Its responses to the market are insensitized. And what is not less important: its production serves to augment the numerator as well as the denominator of the crucial Taxation/Marketed Output proportion that determines the impact of taxation on price.

Because of this entropy build-up, it is no longer enough for social critics to make demands upon private industry. They must rise to the responsibilty of enquiring into the ability of the given industry to meet those demands without going under. Or if they are unperturbed by that prospect, the social critics must have thought out how they will replace the industry in question before they make their demands. That is a difficult and troublesome chore that does not always dovetail neatly with the stylistic requirements of politics. And yet it is impossible to run a complex, pluralistic economy steering by the assumptions of a dead century. The old clichés and marching songs are not enough.

---

redistributing income from higher to lower income groups. (*The Intellectual Capital of Michal Kalecki,* the University of Tennessee Press, Knoxville, 1975, p. 174).

The relative effectiveness of these three techniques will have changed drastically with the altered distribution in our society – not only as between workers and entrepreneurs, but as between the private and the public sectors.

Interacting one with another, these gathering entropies have contributed to a pessimism that has come to be felt throughout our society. Hazel Henderson has captured the sepia mood that is enveloping us:

'Simply put, the entropy state is a society at the state when complexity and interdependence have reached such unmanageable proportions that the transaction costs equal or exceed its productive capabilities. In a manner analogous to physical systems, the society winds down of its own weight and the proportion of its gross national product that must be spent in mediating conflicts, controlling crime, footing the bill for all the social costs generated by the "externalities" of production and consumption, providing ever more comprehensive bureaucratic coordination and generally trying to maintain "social homeostasis" begins to grow exponentially. Such societies may have already drifted to a soft landing in a steady state, with inflation masking their declining condition.

'We must face the fact that business cycles in these mature industrial economies are created by economists and governments rather than by market forces and therefore market forces can no longer be relied on to right things. . . . As any citizen who watched President Ford's inflation summit knows, economics has become a substitute for thought.'

The paper from which this excerpt is taken is entitled 'The End of Economics'.[10]

Not the least of Hazel Henderson's merits is having extended the entropy concept from purely physical to social relationships. And yet she has missed an important aspect of the entropy pattern: there is not one but many entropies – both in the material world and in society. What they have in common is that they all involve waning differences of potential, and because of that there may always exist the possibility of draughting one to revitalize another that is failing. Indeed the very upheavals that hasten the erosion of potential differences of one kind bring completely new ones into existence elsewhere. With an adequate understanding of our entropy problems, we will find in such new negentropies the means of managing our future. In entitling her provocative paper 'The End to Economics', Ms. Henderson would seem locked in a single entropy system. For surely we shall have need of a relevant economic theory to teach us the nature of our entropies and to guide

10 From *Technological Forecasting and Social Change* (American Elsevier Publishing Co. Inc., New York, 1976).

us in our complex world.

Let me illustrate the point with an example of such a new negentropy thrown up by our altered economic topography. Though conventional economic theory works hard at ignoring it, a structural price gradient has sprung up in our society. Were we to recognize it, we could employ it as a negentropy source both to moderate its own slope and to harness it for socially desirable ends. But before you can exploit the drop of a river, you must admit to yourself that it is there.

Our price gradient has put fixed investments in a special position: they are not reproducible at their historic cost. A quasi-rent somewhat in the Marshallian sense becomes incorporated into their value. Let us coin the term 'Structural Quasi-Rent (SQR) to denote this. The phenomenon, of course, has nothing to do with the time-lag in producing capital goods that underlies the Marshallian quasi-rent.[11] It emerges rather because the goods in question were produced in a previous *temporal cost zone*. We must, in fact, train ourselves to think in terms of temporal cost zones. When we have done so, much that appears baffling about our economy will become clear.

Essentially SQR brings in more distant horizons to redress the balance of today's markets. Under its influence capacity for current supply is created in response to future demand – to profit by the economies arising from the creation of as yet unrequired capacity in temporal cost zone t_0. The additional supply available at t_1 as a result of this increment of capacity will tend to depress price at t_1. Moreover, when its output is actually needed at t_a, this additional capacity built at t_0 will incorporate into the price at t_a components of costs as they existed at t_0, and thus will tend to keep prices somewhat lower at that point than they would otherwise have been. Of course, the prices charged at t_a will make some allowance for the higher replacement costs of the fixed capital at that moment; but the net result will still be lower than it would have been had the extra capacity been built only at t_a when it was needed. SQR will thus contribute to keep prices lower at both t_1 and t_a.

Such foresight, I suppose, could be classified as an imperfection of the market, but it is highly useful to society. Indeed, part of our problem has been that economic decisions in the political sector are too often made with a time horizon set by the next election, while equilibrium theory has canonized zero visibility as a norm.

---

11 Alfred Marshall, *Principles of Economics,* Macmillan & Co. Limited, London, 1936. pp. 622-8.

In addition to its contribution in reducing the price gradient, SQR is a source of negentropy for the Keynesian subsystem. With an assured prospect of higher replacement costs for their fixed capital investment, entrepreneurs are more prepared to risk the growing uncertainties closing in on them from the other entropy systems.

The entrepreneur balances present losses due to an excess of capacity against the prospects of future gain through SQR. This gives rise to a forward tilt throughout the economy that it would be dangerous to ignore. For with our economic activities assuming such posture, they can easily be thrown off balance.

If L is the average slope of the price gradient during the life of a capital good, its average value per unit will be $\frac{(1+L)^{n+1}-1}{nL}$ and hence the average SQR will be that amount less unity or

$$\frac{(1+L)^{n+1}-nL-1.}{nL}$$

SQR brings into being a distinct sort of 'producer's surplus'. The storing of lower costs from earlier zones calls for special entrepreneurial flair and daring. It is not unreasonable that the public sector, in its great need, should wish to recapture some of the advantages deriving from SQR; above all since, for the better or the worse, its spending is largely responsible for the price gradient. In effecting such recapture, however, the state must be careful not to destroy the motivations for the continued creation of SQR. The negentropy of the SQR system must be respected.

SQR must not be confused with profit. If the investment incorporating the SQR goes unused, not only will the SQR be lost in whole or in part, but so, too, may a portion of the original investment. The greater the mass of our long-term investment – human as well as material, public as well as private – and the steeper our price gradient, the greater the loss will be from such idle capacity. This suggests how great the cost to society of the periodic deflating of our economies by misconceived 'stabilization' policy.

Only when it is realized, does SQR become profit. Even then, by taxing as profits part of the replacement costs of fixed capital, governments run the risk not only of undermining the motivations for the further production of SQR, but of stripping society of its capital stock. There is, however, no way of seeing the reality of such matters if you take price stability as your creed, and view any price movement as a temporary aberration.

Years ago many businessmen came to realize that a secular price gradient had come into being in our economy; it has been the prospect of SQR that kept many industries expanding. A great deal of industrial, commercial and residential building, for example, went on long before the additional capacity was needed. And on such empty space governments, as a rule, collected taxes. In multiple ways the price gradient has been a major source of negentropy that kept our economy going. It would be an enlightening exercise to reconstruct the performance of our economy over the past decade on the supposition that price stability had been achieved and maintained. What would emerge would be anything but an edifying picture.

The price gradient relieved the public sector of much of the burden of keeping the Keynesian subsytem satisfied: entrepreneurs made far more investments than the Keynesian 'accelerator' effect (based on effective, current demand) would in itself warrant. It also produced substantial revenues to the state through taxes on the income generated by this additional economic activity and on the unused productive capacity that resulted.

Wish the price gradient away, and the call on the state to keep the Keynesian subsystem satisfied would grow. The tax-base on which this increased volume of taxes would have to be raised would shrivel. This would in itself tend to restore in some degree the price gradient that we had wished away.

The price gradient is in fact not likely to be gotten rid of in any great hurry. The sooner that we recognize it for what it is – part of the pronounced forward lean that our economy has developed – the better we shall learn to neutralize its injustices and make positive use of it.

Essentially SQR is annual revenue that can be imputed to the appreciated replacement costs of fixed capital. When such imputed revenue in turn is capitalized, we have an accretion of capital – in money terms – of similar order to that of the original investment. Since this can serve as security for further borrowing that can in turn be invested in anticipation of further SQR, a highly-levered inflationary potential does lurk in the SQR pattern. There is, too, the likelihood that such unconventional insights into the effects of the price gradient are likely to come first to the more venturesome.

Received economic theory, denying the existence of a price gradient, can shed little light on such SQR. Intuitively, however, bankers have sensed this unlimited potential for micro-expansion opened up by the price gradient. By anticipating society's capital needs and profiting by the price gradient, it is in theory possible for a firm to escalate its assets far beyond what is normal in the routine course of business. Unchecked, this could not only outstrip conceivable demand for years ahead, but the available resources in labor and materials.Moreover, such virtuoso leverage of borrowing would place a disproportionate part of the risk on the shoulders of the lenders. Nonetheless, with a relevant theory governments would be equipped to take precautions against such dangers, and still allow the economy to benefit fully from the utilization of SQR.

Still other negentropies that we may draw upon are suggested by our counter-culture. As it develops and deepens, the pluralism of our society will not be confined to demands for greater revenue shares within the established framework of values. Foreseeably, it will bring the legitimization of new value codes and life styles that will redefine the relationship between man and his material possessions. Up to now the operational word in our pluralism has been 'confrontation'; and confrontations we have had with everybody and everything with but a single exception – with the cold arithmetic of accountancy. We can only hope that the era of confrontation will give way to an era of symbiosis of different value codes. From the standpoint of an entropy-menaced society the 'dropping out' of a portion of our younger generation to follow less materially-oriented paths should no longer be seen as a desertion or a betrayal. On the contrary, it could help us live within our dwindling energy and other resources. It could be regarded, moreover, as a hothouse for alternatives. And in the final analysis the availability of alternatives is the most important of all negentropies. That, too, I will explore in a later chapter.[12]

---

12 Though negentropy can be piped in from different systems, it is not to be assumed that the law of composition is always that of simple addition. Each entropy system in fact depends upon a social phenomenon which may have many different facets. By tapping a new system we may be bringing in not only the potential difference upon which our interest is focussed, but still others that may have an important unscheduled effect.

Thus by the latter 1980's we can foresee a drop in the birth rate and family formation in Canada as we see the end of the echo at a generation's distance of the jump in birth rates and immigration after the last World War. This presents a demographic entropy build-up that is bound to have serious economic consequences; we can confidently predict a dramatic jump in immigration at that time to meet it. However, this immigration is likely to contain a higher proportion of manual laborers than is prevalent among the native Canadian population. As a result, it will bring an easing or even a reversal of the first entropy build-up that I discussed above. The filling of a population gap by immigration will thus have an unscheduled counterentropic effect in a different entropic system.

Chapter Five

Policy Operators – the Tablets from the Mount

I have charted the subsystems and entropies of our economy; but before we can proceed to a discussion of policy, we still have an important step to take.

Policies are not fashioned directly from fundamental economic theory. Instead the decision-makers of the practical world draw upon a store of pre-packaged concepts to serve them as building-blocks. These I will call *policy operators.*

Policy-makers rarely have the time or background to examine the validity of the concepts with which they work. They have them on faith and hearsay. Policy operators can be likened to the tablets handed down from Sinai for the guidance of those below. Pure theory, on the other hand, is something that occurs on top of the mountain itself. It is not given to many mortals to enter into the proceedings at that level.

Practical folk deal with these operators as though they were the ultimate scientific truth. They are unaware that there is in fact no ultimate scientific truth – only crucial aspects of a changing reality that can be caught in appropriate conceptual structures. From these alone can useful policy operators be deduced.[1]

---

1 We could call the level of thought occupied by such policy operators 'the K plane '– after Keynes, of course, and perhaps also after Michal Kalecki. 'In 1933, outside the mainstream of traditional economic theory an unknown Polish economist, without formal training in economics, brought up almost exclusively on Marx and influenced by the writings of Rosa Luxemburg, without any contact with Keynes, was able to anicipate Keynes by a full three years in creating a system that contains everything of importance in the Keynesian system, in addition to other contribution. . . .' (Lawrence R. Klein, *The Life of John Maynard Keynes,* Journal of Political Economy, October, 1951).

While in Poland, let us note the unusual case of Oskar Lange, distinguished

Elsewhere[2] I have examined the relativistic nature of all theory. It concentrates our attention on those features of the economy that its authors consider decisive. They do this by choosing an angle of vision, a time horizon, a portion of the field of reality, and a focal length for our perceptions. They achieve their goal in this way by shutting out part of reality. Basic economic theories have always in fact derived as much of their importance from what they shut out as from what they included in their vision.

In this way Adam Smith's Invisible Hand was hardly a portrayal of anything that existed in any society. But it did provide a powerful tool for clearing the terrain of the feudal restrictions that stood in the way of capitalist development. Smith, indeed, made use of at least three distinct value theories and shifted from one to another with a complete lack of self-consciouness as he directed his attention to different problems.

Marginal theory shut out all of reality that did not fit into its idealized market logic. It went further: it absorbed the whole economic process into a single mathematical device, and thus rendered its theory crustacean. To the layman its intimidating mathematical shell seemed the very essence of high science that brooks no appeals.

More than ever, that deepened the gap between fundamental theory and the policy operators. Only academic economists could really know what went on in the halls of pure economic science, and they were not given to ventilating their doubts before laymen. Not until it became impossible to go on ignoring it, would they pay any heed to unorthodox reality. As a result of all this, society was committed to very costly hindsight in dealing with the changes that took place in the economy. And our era has been one of profound changes.

There is no adequate way of adapting policy to a radically transformed economy without rethinking fundamental theory. Altering our policy operators alone will not be enough.

That has indeed become the tragedy of Keynes in our day. He fashioned an effective set of policy operators to deal with the problems of the Depression – such concepts as aggregate demand, liquidity preference, deficit financing. His introspections on the fundamental theoretical level, however, were fragmentary and essentially private.

---

economist who adhered to marginal value theory, and later a high official of the Communist state was presumably able to reconcile this fundamental theory with a set of quite alien policy operators.

2 op. cit. pp. 120 et seq.

Though he did cut it back to the ground, he left marginal theory with its roots intact. In due time it was bound to sprout a new crop of the same old, noxious weed. It was in this way that the Neo-Keynesians contrived to reduce Keynes's ideas to an offshoot of equilibrium theory. More incredible still, they misused his policy operators to persuade governments to push interest rates to all-time highs in pursuit of an equilibrium which for Keynes was non-existent. And increasingly people are blaming Keynes for the disastrous consequences of such policies.

The failure of a fundamental theory may arise from its not spanning that portion of the field of reality where crucial forces are at work. That is the case of the pure market model with respect both to the Social Lien and Social Revalorization. Under the influence of such a theory, our minds will be as closed to the real significance of such phenomena as the human ear is to frequencies out of its range. Or, again, the model may span the pertinent portion of the field, but be unfittingly structured to register the phenomenon. Its effect may be locked up in a catch-all coefficient, and our attention riveted to quite irrelevant variables and patterns.

Let me demonstrate such perverse interpretations of belatedly recognized 'facts' that flow from an inappropriate fundamental model. For the purpose I will go back to the set of truisms assembled by John Hotson that I already utilized in an earlier chapter.

$P \equiv V(M/Q) \equiv GNP/Q \equiv C+I+G+(X-m)/Q \equiv k(W/Q) \equiv h(B/Q) \equiv j(S/Q)$.

Choose any of these and misinterpret them to be causal equations. Once you have adjusted your logic to its structures, some inescapable consequence ensue.

1) $P \equiv V(M/Q)$. In simplified form this is the monetarist model. V (velocity) is assumed frozen, and assimilated into the landscape. In real life, however, it is a very mercurial factor. Your vision will be focussed on identifying 'inflation' with an excess of M, the money supply. In this setting, let us assume that the fact has finally gotten through to you that an increase in taxation, too, is somehow associated with price rise. Within the bounds of this model this can mean only one thing: the government is financing its 'excess' of spending by adding to the money supply. This may or may not be the case. In either instance it does not touch the real heart of the matter.

It fails, for example, to consider the case of a relative expansion of the public sector financed by a balanced budget and accompanied by shrinkage of the private sector through deflation. In that case the total money supply and, indeed, total demand would remain constant or actually shrink. By the insights of the simplistic monetarist model this should lead to a stable price level. In actual fact, if enough taxes were collected from the deflated price sector to pay for the expansion of the public sector, you might even have a drop in the price level initially due to the ruin and liquidation of many businesses. Yet when the dust settled, other things being equal, the price level would have to be higher because of the broader layer of taxation per unit price. Once business was permitted to return to normal operations prices would have to cover this.

None of this is discernible in terms of the model in question: it is outside its field. It completely disregards the negentropies of the private sector. Pushing down the price level by any means is mistaken for progress towards equilibrium. Essentially it is a stylization of the old trade cycle. Our prices today move upward in large part due to structural changes of the economy. There is no way of tracking shifts in the ratio of public to private sector in this model.

2) $P \equiv C + I + G + (X - m)/Q$.

($C =$ consumption; $I =$ Investment; $G =$ Government Expenditure.
$X =$ Exports; $m =$ imports – all in dollars;
$Q =$ physical quantity of output).

This equation is a veritable magician's hat from which you can extract all sorts of rabbits; the only prerequisite is that your audience have long enough ears. By right-handed causality, for example, you find that inflation is due to any of the following, depending upon which variable your fancy happens to alight upon: 'too many dollars chasing too few goods', 'too much investment', 'too much government', or 'too much export trade'. Or if you are left-handed in your causality, you can see in rising prices the cause of increased consumption ('let's buy our colored televisions before prices go up still more'), excessive investment, or too much government expenditure (a fragmentary truth).

To illustrate how dangerous such 'mathematical' reasoning can be, higher prices can even be taken as a means of *improving* our trade balance! All that is needed is to assume C, I, and G to be constant and apply left-handed causality and you have $dP \equiv d(X - m)/Q$. What is more, it is actually true *up to a point:* increased prices for our exports would improve our terms of trade (other things being equal – which would not be the case for very long). The overriding effect of such a domestic price increase would be the worsening, not the improvement, of our trade balance. But we have simply banished the other relationships from our field by assuming them to be constant.

The causal structures of reality have been eliminated in our model, the relationships flattened out. A scholastic drilling has trained economists to think not in terms of cause and effect circuits with complex feedbacks, but of mutual, self-balancing relationships. We have fallen victim to a set of policy operators that have little connection with the real world.

The equilibrium operator has taken command of all mainstream economic thinking, whether monetarist, Neo-Keynesian, or Galbraithian. Each starts out with the unquestioned premise that price stability is not only feasible, but must be our top priority. From there on they go each his own way in attributing the perverse performance of the economy to his favorite villian – too much money supply, too much aggregate demand, to the power structures of the market, and so forth. Like empty vending machines their researches deliver only the small coin they have put in.

Let us proceed to formulate a set of policy operators derived from the foregoing chapters that are relevant to our contemporary problems.

1. *Price is a summation.* Its components originate in the various subsystems of the economy. It cannot therefore be deduced *a priori* by any one logic. To ascertain what prices should be, we cannot take as our point of departure the requirements of a stable price level. If we did, we should end up applying the wrong arithmetical operation – division in order to establish the cost components, rather than the addition of those cost components in order to arrive at the end price. And once we apply the wrong arithmetic operation in dealing with the problems of price, there is simply no limit to the amount of grief that we will get ourselves into. That is in fact just what happened during the past decade.

Businessmen, of course, have always made a practice of *adding* their costs to calculate the price they put on their wares. Because they did this instead of maximizing their profits, theoretical economists held the belief that they really did not understand what they were doing. It is time that economists realized that it was they who were without a clue as to how the market operated. More than ever in our pluralistic economy, price determination has become a matter of addition. Our policy-making must be based upon a recognition of this.

2. *'Labor's real wage' must be conceived as including the basket of unpriced services that it receives from the state.*

As commonly used, the crucial concept 'real wage' is identified with labor's take-home pay adjusted to the consumer's price index. Occasionally labor's complete wage with the same adjustment is taken for the purpose.[3]

Either of these notions omits the full cost of the growing basket of public services. For that cost includes not only the direct taxes that we ourselves pay, but the growing layer of taxation in price. As a result of this error our attitude towards unpriced public services is very much that of children receiving gifts from Santa Claus. And because of that, like children at Christmas, we have developed a way of asking for more and more of such public services. Had we, however, been trained to keep track of the full cost to us of public services, we would not allow politicians to bribe us with our own money.

We must then learn to carry out the 'full costing' of public services: more taxation *plus* a component of price increase through higher taxation in price. Unless we do so, we shall be unequipped to make rational decisions concerning our public services. Certain public services may be judged desirable even though they do entail a higher price level. An electorate may choose public dental insurance over an increase in the private output of cigarettes or bubble gum, even though the former would contribute to a higher price level and the latter to a lower one. It would after all be ironical if a dogma that began by reducing all economics to the maximization of consumer satisfactions, ended up by denying the consumer the freedom of informed choice on such matters.[4]

3. *Private enterprise must be seen as a tool rather than an ideology.*

We must learn to step out of the last-century debate on public vs. private enterprise. In our day the private sector could not operate

3 'The increase in real wages is measured by the difference between the nominal wage increase and the growth in the cost of living'. Economic Council of Canada, Thirteenth Annual Review *The Inflation Dilemma,* Minister of Supply and Services, Ottawa, 1976, p. 25.

'In Canada real after-tax income per person more than doubled in the thirty years following World War II' *Working Paper – The Way Aheads A Framework for Discussion,* Government of Canada, Ottawa, 1976, p. 10.

4 More is involved than just the absolute amount of the withdrawal of purchasing power via the social lien. Its manner of distribution stands in contrast with that of taxation. In theory the burden of taxation to pay for the public services we are demanding may be isolated to affect a few social groups. There is hope that the other fellow will be stuck with the taxation, while we ourselves will enjoy the services it goes to pay for. This is not the case with the higher price level arising from added social services via the social lien. That strikes the entire population. Indeed, unless it is compensated for, its effect is likely to be regressive.

without physical and social infrastructures that only the state can provide. On the other hand, the experiences on both sides of the Iron Curtain have shown governments to be poor and even non-performers in many areas. We must therefore seek the most productive combination of private and public enterprise for the task at hand. That, however, will be impossible so long as we remain mired in the grand debate on private enterprise vs. socialism as rival philosophies.

4. *Subsidies do not necessarily restore the negentropy of the private sector.*

Where society decides that it has need of private enterprise for a given task, it must respect the conditions necessary for entrepreneurs to function adequately. Bureaucrats labor under the misconception that whatever the damage they have inflicted on the private sector, it can all be set right again by a big enough subsidy. That not only assuages their conscience, but it feeds their sense of power.

What is decisive for the health of the private sector is not the amount of money injected or extracted by government, but how such intervention occurs, how it affects the functional circuits of private enterprise, the means, motivations, and the capacity for effective decision-making of the entrepreneur.

A subsidy, no matter how generous, may be ruinous to these. It may transfer the essential decision – the conditions for the granting of the subsidy – from the entrepreneur to the bureaucrat. It can rob the former of the sensitivities to the market and the disciplines of risk. From a sharp-nosed negentropy scout, he may become degraded to a fat and lazy retainer of the public sector.

5. *An overall accountancy constraint exists into which all subsystems must fit.*

As relative as are the perceptions of any social group, in every society it is given to one particular group to concern itself with the overall accountancy constraints under which the whole economy operates. As a rule this is the group that is left with the economic residue after distribution has taken place. It pays the bills and performs the account-balancing function. In different societies this function is entrusted to different classes. No one group is irreplaceable in the role: it is the role itself that cannot be done away with. But it can be overlooked. That, indeed, is close to the roots of our present difficulties.[5]

---

5 The reference here is strictly to accountancy constraints. The physical constraints of the ecological system will be primarily the concern of the public sector.

It is a disturbing feature of our contemporary scene that this account-balancing role is to a large extent divorced from the political institutions and the social groups in the hands of which power is increasingly concentrated. For at bottom that account-balancing function is our mooring to reality. The failure of economic theory, moreover, has left us without a serviceable unit for our social accounting. The benchmarks of a previous age are no adequate substitute.

Much of our malaise stems from our disregard of the structure of quantitative constraint that underlies the very concept of distribution. There is evidence of this in the very etymology of the word – the Latin *tribuo,* allot or assign, that is related to the root 'three'. That reminds us that originally the Romans were divided into three tribes *(tribus,* the dative of *tres).* Even in ancient Rome, however, such matters were subject to constant change, and the three tribes in time ended up as thirty-five. It would thus have been impossible to go on apportioning duties and revenues on the basis of three tribes, though that primeval arithmetic remained lodged in the word 'distribute'.[6]

We likewise must avoid carrying over concepts of distribution corresponding to dead periods that are imbedded in our inherited ideologies.

The scope for inter-family distribution was severely limited in early societies. Just keeping metabolism going was a major effort, survival an achievement. Essentially distribution implies a degree of leisure and freedom from such concerns. When a surplus that could be translated into leisure appeared, it was concentrated in the hands of those groups who performed specialized functions for the community – priests and warriors. As social structures changed, that surplus, varying in size, shifted to different groups; but it continued in the possession of the privileged classes.

Our economic theory came into being in a world that conformed to this general pattern. And yet something novel had already made its appearance. Modern technology had begun expanding the surplus at a quickening pace, though initially the living standards of the masses were not greatly altered.That is why most 19th century economic theories made some very ready assumptions about the availability of a disposable economic surplus for redistribution. These assumptions are not necessarily tenable in our own time.

---

6 Charlton T. Lewis and Charles Short, *A Latin Dictionary,* Oxford University Press, Oxford, 1879, under *tribuo* and *tribus.*

We have, for example, already noted that Marx's system rested on the gap between the time it took the worker to produce new value equal to the wages paid him, and to replace the capital consumed, and his total working hours. That was the cornucopia upon which the system rested.

Since Marx's day society has undergone much change. A goodly portion of society's quantum of leisure – once the monopoly of the upper classes – has come to be apportioned to the workers. Not only is there a shorter working day, holidays, longer schooling, earlier retirement and the coffee-break, but even such enforced leisure as unemployment *with* unemployment insurance benefits. The state too, drains off a substantial portion of the surplus produce to redistribute according to its wisdom. Given all this, a new pattern emerges. We can no longer assume out of hand that the cornucopia is still there and that there is still enough in it to draw upon. There may well be, of course. But that calls for verification – like checking the gasoline in the tank of your car. For even if that cornucopia is not empty today, we need only extrapolate what has been going on to realize that we cannot be sure that it will not be empty tomorrow. However, the postures of most liberal and leftist parties are based on just such an assumption. In their redistributionalist policies they assume that the tribes of Rome are still three.

Nor is this type of error confined to the left. It underlies the equilibrium model that imprisons our thinking on economic subjects. This makes two assumptions:

1) The economic activities of the state continue so minor that they may safely be dismissed as 'exogenous'; the burden of their cost on price can be more than made good by increased productivity so that a stable price level continues to be feasible.

2) The increased well-being of the masses and the transformation of our economy into a service economy can be counterbalanced in their effect on price by this same mounting productivity. This presupposes expanding mass-production of commodities on an ever more power-intensive basis. What is overlooked is the constraints of our resources system which are asserting themselves in a dramatic way. .We run the risk of being gored on the legendary cornucopia, upended to emphasize how little is left in it.

For our conventional economists, too, the tribes of Rome are still three: the traditional distribution model blinds them to our present-day realities.

We are, in short, trapped in vintage concepts of endless reserves of leisure and surplus. Only on such premises could the priorities of our reigning theories be realized. Once we discard such assumptions, disconcerting things start happening. Firm pillars give way, and imposing vaults overhead threaten to fall in. Our models have simply been trying to extract more from the economy than has been put into it. It does not matter how hallowed the theory, or how smashing the majority of the party elected to translate it into policy. We have come up against constraints of arithmetic that have the elasticity of a brick wall.

And when arithmetic declines to yield, other things will – notably prices and interest-rates, those anchor-bolts of the received economic models. With that, completely unforeseen counter-redistributional effects start occurring throughout the economy. The recognition of the inevitability of this is important enough for us to elevate it to the rank of policy operator:

6) *Policy based on a model at variance with the constraints of reality must give rise to uncheduled counter-redistributional effects.*

More than anything else this is undermining the morale of our society – not so much the price rise in itself, but a price rise not foreseen and misinterpreted when it takes place. If it were understood, not only could the price gradient be compensated for, but governments could make good use of it for policy ends.

7) *The structural price gradient must be included as a basic datum in all planning.* Ignoring it must be regarded as crude an error as an architect who drew his plans without surveying the slope of the site. The price gradient must not only be predicted, but reduced into its main components. Only by such a conscious attempt to understand our economic topography can we have meaningful policy design.

8) *Properly analysed, the price and interest-rate gradients can open up powerful economic negentropies for policy-making.*

The interest-rate gradient – a differential function of the price gradient of higher order – calls for special attention under this heading. For long-term interest-rates help determine the uses to which we can put society's capital. The changing forms assumed by our society's capital accumulation have serious feedbacks into the interest-rate that have been neglected by economists.

The transformations that our economy is undergoing can only be compared to mankind's transition from the palaeolithic to the neolithic age some seven or eight thousand years ago. At that time a series of inventions changed human existence from a haphazard day-to-day affair to permit the storing of reserves. The domestication of animals lessened dependence on hunting; agriculture came to displace the gathering of wild fruits and seeds; pottery provided storage; and above all the development of writing opened the way for conserving knowledge. For the first time society acquired a 'fly-wheel'.[7]

Western civilization has long been an accumulating culture, but in our times the nature of that accumulation has changed in radical ways. Its center of gravity has been shifting from chattels to information, in essence to a type of storage of higher order.

The stress of the Protestant ethic had been laid on the storing up of ducats in private purses. Today neither the Protestant ethic, ducats, nor private purses are remotely what they used to be. Monetary gold has given way to what is somewhat optimistically termed 'managed money'. The leakage of social lien and other structural components into price has resulted in currencies of very mobile purchasing power. Private ownership itself has become a qualified institution.

Society's major accumulation lies increasingly outside the private sector – in the public sector or straddling the two. The knowledge and training paid for by the state are lodged in private heads – though they do make up an increasingly significant portion of society's capital accumulation. And all aspects of this new social accumulation contribute to our structural price gradient.

Even though it is diffusely situated, the dimensions of this capital formation have grown spectacularly. This has been further accentuated by the population explosion which must itself been seen as a by-product of our accumulation of knowledge. To finance all this, the world is faced with a capital famine of traumatic proportion.

9) A policy operator of importance emerges from this: *Deflationary policy – whether to stabilize price, currency or what not – must be harmful at a time when capital creation is a fundamental need to safeguard society's future.* Imposing idleness on people who wish to work, or leaving productive capacity underemployed cannot be justified. We have left behind us the Keynesian era when *any* sort of activity was better than none. The entropies of our resources system impose a purposeful direction and timing on our economic activities.

10) *The price gradient has made of credit a powerful tool of re-*

7 The expression belongs to Georges Charbonneau and appears in his *Entretiens avec Claude Lévi-Strauss,* Paris, 1961, p. 30.

distribution.

Credit has always been the manna in the private enterprise system. To those to whom it was available it opened up endless opportunities. During crises, commanding even short-term loans could make the difference between ruin and speculative bonanza.

The development of a structural price gradient reinforces this benign power of credit. Their addiction to a theory that denies the existence of a structural price gradient has prevented governments from recognizing this elementary fact – the price gradient is certainly one of the most effective redistributional mechanisms of our period. Over the past generation, millions have found that buying a home with a large mortgage enabled them to build up a greater equity than they could have accumulated through a lifetime of saving.

Recognition of this must occupy a prominent place in the arsenal of policy tools of any government.[8]

From all sides the evidence is streaming in upon us that our economy is sick with the mania of bigness. The pressure on our resources system, the price gradient itself, the unthinking worship of GNP statistics, are but some of the symptoms. I have dealt with some of these phenomena individually. Now I will venture upon a generalized mathematical reorientation to help us with this problem.

When we have learned to do our economic thinking in terms of negentropy and subsystem logics, it will become apparent that in every instance there is a critical ratio that holds the key to our problem. It will serve us as a control gauge to measure the pertinent entropy accumulation. In given areas of the resources subsystem this be may the energy costs of producing new fuel as a proportion of the new fuel produced; in many problems relating to the private sector it will be the Structural Quotient in the economy – the relative size of the public

8 Let no one recoil from my suggestion of building policy about a price gradient that conventional theory sees as a pathological symptom. Those whose readings of history extend beyond the celebrated German inflation of the early twenties will be aware that price movement played an important part in fashioning our institutions over the past millenium and more. Marc Bloch has this to say about the conversion of investiture rights owed the feudal lord into cash: 'On the other hand, where these assessments (connected with the investiture) were set in currency once for always – the outstanding example is in the English Magna Charta – the obligation was finally hit by that progressive erosion from the 12th century to our modern times, 'was to be the inevitable fate of all obligations fixed in perpetuity'. (La Société Féodale, Editions Albin Michel, Paris, 1939, p. 320

sector to the economy as a whole.

11) *To deal with such crucial ratios, we must learn to do more of our economic reasoning in terms of net effect; we must train ourselves in the methods of modular congruence arithmetic.*

When two functions are congruent to modulus k, their difference is divisible by k. They are written $f(x) \equiv g(x) \pmod{k}$. They are each made up of a multiple of k plus the same remainder. In this calculus it is the common remainder that is alone of importance.[9] Without realizing it, we make frequent use of congruence algebra in our everyday life. Thus in our names for the days of the week we employ a congruence arithmetic to modulus 7; starting from Sunday as a base the third, tenth, seventeenth, and twenty-fourth days are equivalent – they are all of them Tuesday.

Applied to economic reasoning modular congruence calculus would focus our attention on the net effect of two inverse operations. It would establish the lemma that only the net effect of the effort is likely to be useful; the multiple of the modulus will probably be contraproductive. By striving to eliminate the multiple of the modulus, we should be increasing our net economic benefits.

Thus *whatever the quantum of public services delivered, it is desirable that the fiscal turn-over be kept to a minimum.* Quite apart from the apparent cost of any state intervention, there is a further cost in terms of various entropy build-ups that must be considered. A policy format in which the state taxes an industry with one hand and subsidizes them with the other must be seen as burdensome. The goal would be to reduce the interventions in contrary senses to their single net effect – to subsidize or to tax in the net amount. Taxing and subsidizing at the same time must be seen as similar to running a heating system against an air-conditioner. By reducing the arrangement to a single net heating or cooling operation, we should be eliminating a double waste of energy.

An other instance of the same modular principle: energy experts tell us that we would be further ahead if we improved the insulation of our buildings and developed correspondingly fewer new sources of fuel. The cost of such insulation is less than the cost of developing new fuel sources to provide us with the fuel that we are wasting

Our oil needs could be expressed by the following modular congrence equation.

---

9 Harris Hancock, *Foundations of the Theory of Algebraic Numbers.* Dover Publications, New York, 1964. Vol. 1, p. 2.

Oil needs ≡ Net Fuel Needs (mod. oil savings due to insulation).

Of course any extensive use of this calculus will lead to a substantial shrinkage of our Gross National Product. Brought about in this way, that will be a good thing. Once we train ourselves to think and perceive in terms of this mathematical format, opportunities to apply it with good effect will turn up in every area of the economy.

Chapter Six

Policy In A Pluralistic Economy

So long as we go on making a fetish of price stability, we will make no progress in managing our economy. Even without a detailed analysis, we could know that the tangle of causalities involved could hardly lead us to such an appointed goal.[1]

We must learn to design our policies around the structural price gradient as the central fact of economic life. Even in the absence of an adequate theory, proposals have begun to be advanced in this sense from many different quarters. Some of these have affinity with some of the ideas of this chapter. Confronted with the problem of survival, practical people are formulating partial solutions long before economists have extricated themselves from their dogma. This is not the first time

---

1 This is not the first time that an irrational taboo has come between society and its real problems. A few years ago Britain's economic managers were prepared to stop at nothing to uphold the exchange rate. 'The politicians' opposition to devaluation in Britain was a mixture of various prejudices. . . . The Labour Party in particular was afraid of being labelled the party of devaluation. . . . But politicians also had an identification of the strength of sterling with the position of Britain in the world, and its role as a world banker. Those who regarded this role as an incubus rather than a benefit were dismissed as people ignorant of the mysteries of high finance. . . And the idea of "honour" was also invoked: devaluation would be the equivalent of a banker dishonouring his his pledges. . . .

'As the chronological account makes clear, three years were occupied in the struggle to avoid devaluation. The Prime Minister committed himself against it to such an extent that civil servants were virtually forbidden to study the possibility, and it became an unmentionable word in Whitehall. . . . When eventually the decision was taken, it was treated by the Chancellor of the day, Mr. Callaghan, as a matter of honour, and he resigned.' (F. Blackaby, *Changes in British Economic Policy,* 1960-73, in *Economic Policies Compared West and East,* Vol. 2, *National and International,* E. S. Kirschen, Editor, North-Holland Publishing Company, Amsterdam, Oxford, 1975, pp. 33 and 34).

that this sort of thing has happened.

That is all for the good; but hardly enough. Our economy has grown so complex, that we cannot rely upon intuition in managing it. Jay W. Forrester has written of the counterintuitive nature of social systems.[2] It is not enough for us just to 'learn to live with inflation'. There is in fact no way of doing so without taking note of the new economic topography that has arisen, and harnessing it imaginatively for positive ends.

What I offer in this chapter and the next is to be taken only as a random sampling of the policy insights that will come from a theory that is relevant to our pluralistic reality.

DETAXATION

Since the injection of growing streams of taxation into price has been partly responsible for our troubles, a simple remedy suggests itself: to bleed as much taxation out of price as possible. Yet such a course cannot be undertaken with our eyes shut. Long ago the novelists of nostalgia taught us that there is no going home. If we turn the hands of our clocks back ten years with respect to a variable or two, that will not necessarily bring our system back to its point of departure.

The variables that we choose for the purpose exist only in a context of still other variables, and these exert their influence only through the logics of the various subsystems. Each of these has a unidirectional, entropic history of its own. In our cures, as in our diagnosis, we must avoid the trap of a monistic logic. Whatever we propose doing in one subsystem must be studied for its probable effects in the other subsystems.

The most obvious flaw in a mechanical policy of detaxation is the very size that the public sector has attained. So dependent have we become upon public services, that even if all waste in the delivery of these were eliminated, the state will still have need of a portion of the national income that would have been unthinkable even ten years ago.

The scope of the detaxation technique must therefore not be limited to the obvious need for ending extravagance and inefficiency. Far more important is the redistribution of the tax burden in ways that would be less damaging to enterprise. To the extent that we are able to revitalize the private sector in this way, we not only enlarge our tax base and lighten the specific burden of social lien in price. We may, too, make

---

2 *Collected Papers of Jay W. Forrester,* Wright-Allen Press, Inc., Cambridge, Mass. 1975, p. 215.

it possible for the public sector to vacate entire areas of the economy where the short-sighted zeal of the tax-collector has put the entrepreneur out of business.

Such a proposal must not be faulted by entrenched ideological judgment. It is not directed against the public sector. If we manage with less public sector where it can be replaced advantageously by private enterprise, it will be possible to direct more public services where they may be irreplaceable and really needed.

It has been one of our great misfortunes that Keynesian theory should have served to reinforce a failing of tax-collectors. From time immemorial governments have tended to satisfy their hungers in the manner most convenient to themselves. Then came Keynesian economics with its emphasis on aggregates. In the setting of the 1930's it was a revolutionary step forward, but it contributed to the self-indulgence not only of lazy-minded economists, but of lazy-minded bureaucrats. Our well-being was seen to depend only upon the balance of aggregate supply and demand. How the latter might bedistributed between the public and private sectors, or even among the various industries, seemed of little moment. And since public services were redressing some ancient injustices, the cost of these services could not be conceived as harmful. Didn't Keynes, after all, dream up the most whimsically useless schemes to illustrate his point that *any* increase in state spending was helpful in getting the economy moving again? Everything, in short, conspired to confirm to the tax-collector that he could do no evil.

After World War II the Neo-Keynesian model made matters even worse. Under cover of a fog of mathematics, it smuggled back the notion of a self-balancing market. And when prices persisted in climbing, the conclusion was that providence had to be helped by jacking up taxes and interest rates. Supposedly this 'syphoned off' purchasing power.

Now we are finally coming to recognize that taxation can not only contribute to price rise, but that the manner of its distribution can undermine private enterprise. It would be helpful if finance ministers were required to commit to memory the entropy buildups that threaten the private sector; they might even be required to recite these at their swearing-in ceremonies. With such preparation, they might avoid taxing an industry out of existence, only to find that the state must step in to replace it, usually at a far higher cost.[3] When this occurs, the new

3 'There is a sort of empirical generalization that it costs the state twice as much to do anything as it costs private enterprise, whatever it is. My son once

demands upon the treasury exceed by far the taxation that put the private industry out of business. And its elimination narrows the tax base that must support the swollen burden of taxation. Very early sailors learn not spit into the wind. The training of our economic policy-makers is less rigorous.

Elsewhere I have examined in detail the absence of a serious depreciation policy for public investment in human and physical capital.[4] So long as higher taxation was seen as conducive to stable prices, paying for long-term investment out of current revenue was considered an overdose of virtue. Once we recognize the social lien effect upon price, we can no longer take that view.

Though paid for out of current income, much of the state's expenditure for health and education will be contributing more to productivity a generation from now than much physical capital that we carefully amortize on private balance sheets. The concept of productive investment by the state does, of course, have blurred edges; this reflects the fact that it is by political process that we decide what is useful and what is wasteful in this area. To make such decisions intelligently, however, the public must have the guidance of an economic theory that would spell out the full costs of public expenditure – not only in taxation but in its effect on price. This it has not had.

The existence of large amounts of unamortized public investment suggests that there is elbow-room for further government borrowing. First, however, we must convince ourselves that this would serve a useful purpose in helping us manage our price gradient. The situation, indeed, is strikingly parallel to that of the thirties. Despite the prejudices rooted in outmoded theory, Keynes was finally able to convince govern-

---

called my attention to this generalization and it is amazing to see how accurate it is. Some studies have been done in the United States on the productivity in handling accounts of people in the governmental social security system and in the private insurance system and private commercial insurance agencies and lo and behold, the ratio of productivity was 2:1.' Milton Friedman in an unnamed book published by the Fraser Institute of Vancouver, quoted in the *Globe and Mail* of Toronto, August 22, 1977.

The *Globe and Mail* article continues: 'He (Friedman) would not fiddle around looking for wasteful expenditure – there is waste everywhere and that would require "across the board" cut, with "every department, every office" required to make "statutory" cuts.'

Instead of concerning himself about negentropies and how to reconcile them, Mr. Friedman is waging an ideological warfare against the public enterprisers.

4 Krehm, op. cit., p. 145.

ments that additional public spending would actually help lighten the burden of the national debt, and help the capitalist world back out of its blind alley. He, too, had come to think in terms of gradients, and of the way the economy has of slipping down them with gathering momentum.

TAX-BONDING

Detaxing – thinning out the layers of taxation in price – is bound to leave serious holes in the state's finances. To fill that gap a companion technique is called for – taxbonding.

Certain classes of entrepreneurs would be given the option of subscribing a portion of their taxable income in tax-bonds, long-term government paper bearing interest at a rate substantially below that of the market. Before maturity the price gradient would shrink the real value of such securities very considerably. This would allow the state to recapture a portion of the Structural Quasi-Rents (SQR) in such industries without impairing their ability to go on functioning. The arrangement would thus ensure the liquidity of the public treasury while respecting the negentropies of the private sector.

The money illusion would be enlisted on behalf of greater price stability, and if the program were suitably designed, of greater social equity. What is involved, in fact, is more than a money illusion. Businessmen are accustomed to operating within different time horizons; nor is it always the most distant horizon that they can afford to steer by. Such taxbonds would offer the entrepreneur important defences in his present menaced setting; in a pinch the bonds could be sold or borrowed against.

If sold, they would, of course, be subject to a discount reflecting the difference between their interest coupons and the market rate. If borrowed against, their value as security would likewise depend upon this factor. Because of this, if a government found that the economy was really 'overheated' – that is, that demand was pressing against the limits of its productive capacity – it could 'cool' it by *lowering* the interest rates on such taxbonds. The idea of fighting real inflation by lowering interest rates is important rather than just picturesque. It would break the vicious spiral of costs that has so shaken the private sector.

What would prompt capitalists to invest profits in taxbonds that were fated to lose some of their real value? Both the uncertainties of the future and an imprecise understanding of the present – two powerful forces in any age. Given our record of economic forecasting, there is no reason to believe that we will have entirely rise above such influences. Moreover, the very prospects of success of the detaxation policy would create the likelihood that our price gradient would be moderated. That would raise hopes of windfall gains amongst those holding taxbonds. Not only do a great variety of theories, appreciations and prejudices obtain in the business world, but a broad spectrum of temperaments to match these.

The discount to which the taxbond would be subject would, moreover, decrease as less of its term remained. The businessman would hope that he would not have to sell his bond at a loss for years to come, or not at all. The same factor, after all, operates in the bond market every day, where investors choose to feel themselves 'locked' in the market.

The funds raised by such taxbonds could be made available by the state in areas of the economy threatened with becoming inoperative because of high interest rates – housing, developments on the frontiers of technology, public utilities, municipal services.

In certain aspects such a tax-bond scheme resembles the investment funds that the tax authorities allow in Sweden. But there is an important difference. In the Swedish plan the funds remain basically with the industry that generates them – though a portion of them is deposited interest-free with the Central Bank until used. Taxbonds, on the other hand, would offer a source of cheap capital for whatever industry the state wished to encourage. In this sense it is a mechanism for capital redistribution. This is of particular importance at a time when much of the financing of large firms takes place internally and thus eludes government policies directed at the capital market.[5]

By combining detaxation with taxbonding, we would in a formal sense be balancing a loss of revenue against increased borrowing by the state – according to traditional wisdom the crimson road to ruin. Once we recognize the structural price gradient, however, and consider the factors that have brought it about, the distinction between revenue and the proceeds of long-term borrowings develops a penumbra. The erosion of the real value of the taxbond will in part reflect the vast expenditures of the state for infrastructures and human capital. The state will thus be recapturing some of the external spill-overs resulting from such

5 Assar Lindbeck, *Swedish Economic Policy,* The Macmillan Press Ltd., London, 1975, p. 98.

outlay. Beyond a doubt it is better for the state to regain some of this advantage, rather than having it go blindly to add to the wealth of the more adroit. That is particularly the case if the method of recapture is designed not to interfere with the functioning of the private sector.

We would be balancing debt that is partly self-liquidating against expenditure by the state. Because of that it would be more appropriate to formulate our fiscal goal as 'budgetary liquidity balance', rather than a balanced budget.

The taxbond could be extended to personal income. It would be possible to incorporate certain insurance features into it to add to its appeal – for example, redemption at par of registered taxbonds upon the death of the holder; or in the event of his lengthy illness or unemployment; or if the money were needed for the purchase of a first house.

Tax-bonding would be geared to taxable income, whereas the taxation foregone would be a high percentage of the taxable income. The net effect on budgetary liquidity would thus be a positive one. It is precisely that net effect that is needed to finance the detaxation policy until the broadening of the tax-base itself is realized by these means.

Would such policies carry with them the danger of runaway inflation? That need not be the case if they were designed around the realities of our pluralistic economy.Not only would the tax-bonds be partly self-liquidating, but the state would come to rely more and more on taxbonds and less on actual taxation. The diminishing burden of taxation in price, and the lower rate of interest in socially necessary industries would keep the price gradient relatively low. The revival of the private sector's negentropies would relieve the state from the need to replace it in many areas of the economy. These influences would interact and snowball. A lesser price gradient along with some popular education in a sounder economic theory would contribute to defuse the so-called 'wage push'.

A self-balancing feedback loop would be established: as the public sector grew in relative magnitude within the economy, the steeper price gradient resulting would increase the prospect of SQR. The expanded scale of economic operations would increase the tax-bond subscriptions and shift more of the burden of financing the state from taxation. This would reduce the price gradient, diminish the prospects of SQR and economic activity. The balance would thus be redressed in favor of taxation.

Society faces the challenge of keeping private enterprise alive and well, but at the same time bridling its inherent drive to exponential expansion. It must learn to direct it where the public interest requires, but without denaturing it. Blind exponential growth is simply not compatible with ecological and resources constraints of our day; and yet we have noted the exponential requirements of the Keynesian subsystem.

To reconcile these contradictory needs, the state must learn to use the levers that pluralistic price theory makes available. Through these it can guide private enterprise without stifling it. It must satisfy the growth requirements of the Keynesian system, but in a way that answers society's needs.

The overall framework into which we must fit our policies is that given by the available energy and non-renewable resources. A severe time dimension is attached to this. The very exponential pattern that technology has given both to demography and economic development imposes lengthy time-leads on our planning.

Though much has been written about this, most policies continue to be improvisations in the political arena. Rarely do they even take us in the general direction in which we know that we should be moving. We are told that 'first we must lick inflation'; but since we have seen that the whole concept of 'licking inflation' is based on a gross error, it follows that in effect we have renounced dealing with those of our problems that really matter.

There is no way of separating our short-term from our long-term problems. More often than not, what we see as short-term problems are nothing more than our long-term problems putting their foot in our door.

To begin with, a matrix of ecological constraints must be set up – in the form of input-output grids not vastly different from those developed by Wassily Leontief. It is within these, and only within these that society's plans must be laid.

Next the Keynesian system must be satisfied. Translated into everyday terms, this means that unemployment must be kept low, and negentropy respected in the private sector. Though an urgent, short-term problem, our mass unemployment must be dealt with only within the constraints of our long-term needs. These needs, after all, are long-term less because they are remote than because it will take us a long time to prepare to meet them. And here the fact that we do have a major unemployment problem can actually be of help to us. The existence of such a crisis means that a fundamental restructuring of our economy is required, and at such times much that is usually rigid in public thinking becomes relatively malleable.

We can not therefore, be satisfied with cranking up the economy to produce still more of what it has been turning out as a means of solving our employment problem. On the other hand crash programs for the development of fuel-saving systems, the insulation of our buildings, the economic recycling of our wastes are obviously in place. Such investments would answer the needs at once of both the Keynesian and the non-renewable resources subsystems. Nor should considerations of price stability stand in the way of our doing this .

Many factors, of course contribute to our unemployment; and not the least of these is a demographic one. The post-war generation is now flooding onto the labor market in great numbers, and on the whole with far greater educational qualifications than their parents brought to it in their day. It does not, however, follow that society can provide them all with the jobs they were trained for: to do so would call for the continued exponential growth of both population and commodity production. We should have to extrapolate into the future the patterns of the past, and our resources subsystem has been warning us that this is not the direction in which we should be moving. We cannot go on multiplying indefinitely our output of bottles and cans just in order to keep the economy going.

But we have also been made aware that the expansion of public services has its pitfalls as well – entropy build-ups that threaten the whole economy with stultification. In their growth both the public and private sectors have landed each in its own blind alley.

What is called for is a new type of collaboration between the two sectors that will reorient our attitudes towards leisure and the quality of life. The general direction would be determined by the government; but for the efficient execution of such projects, the specific talents of private enterprise will have to be enlisted and given full scope. By this new symbiosis it should not only be possible to satisfy the needs of the Keynesian subsystem, but to observe the constraints of our resources system.

Having set up the general purposes of a given program, the state would invite tenders from entrepreneurs for its realization. What would be submitted would be a complete package – both the design of a proposed project and its execution. Those awarded such contracts would be allowed to run them on a profit-and-loss basis. The government would inspect to see that the general specifications are abided by.

Projects of this sort could cover many fields: popular education, recreation, social services, job retraining. In one capacity or another such a program would offer outlets for many of our university graduates for whom there are no openings in the official educational apparatus.

Such a format has quite unlimited possibilities. Our economy is creating on the one hand a growing army of unemployed, inadequately trained workers; and, on the other hand, a huge backlog of neglected maintenance in our cities, not least of all in the very districts where unemployed live. The necessary skill for maintaining these are either in short supply, or are too highly priced to be relevant to their maintenance problems. When parallel problems of cost have arisen in the world of medicine, efforts are being made to create paramedical personnel. These workers relieve medical doctors of many routine tasks and perform them at a far lesser cost. There is no reason why maintenance work left undone because it cannot support the wage rates of highly skilled and highly organized construction workers should not be carried out by unemployed less elaborately trained for the purpose.

The government could call for tenders for fully integrated programs that would include the training of unemployed workers for such purposes, organizing the companies to employ them and to give them their initial working experience. Such programs would be judged fully completed – and thus fully subsidized – when the workers have been kept employed usefully in the given capacity for a year or two. Bringing such a program to a successful conclusion would be a challenge to creative imagination on the part of the employers on several different planes. It would call for degrees of flexibility and dedication, improvisation and personal inventiveness that simply do not flourish in government bureaucracies.

Similar projects could be undertaken to teach homeowners to do much of their maintenance, for social work among the aged, amongst slum-dwellers.

Such a shift from the growth of mass-production of commodities to an increase of personal services would involve some far-reaching changes in our economy. It would bring with it a less dominant position of the large corporation. The concentration of economic power in the hands of a relatively few mammoth corporations has for almost a century been the subject of much public concern in North America and some largely ritualistic legislation. The trend towards bigness is inseparable from an industrial society. Not only do the advantages of scale contribute to this, but the strategies of internal financing that are available only to large corporations. The large corporation, however, by its very nature lacks the sensitivity and pliability needed for the delivery of personal services. And it is only through such personal services, that we can humanize our technological jungle and keep society from falling apart. As the economy is reoriented to the expansion of such services, the trend towards economic concentration will be halted and even reversed.

There would be broad scope for private cultural projects to bring to the average citizen other life-styles than that of consumers of nationally advertised products. Instead of extending its educational bureaucracy, the government could invite proposals for popular educational and recreational projects. Not only would this ensure more satisfactory services at a more economical cost, but it would contribute to keeping the public and private sectors in better balance.

Though at the time they were assailed as boondoggling, many of the W.P.A. projects established under Roosevelt in the United States made important cultural contributions at prices that in retrospect turned out to be bargains – quite apart from their immediate purpose of providing jobs. We have entered a period of similar but far more exacting challenge. Providing enough aggregate demand to start the economy moving again was essentially a quantitative task. Keynes himself underlined that point with his frivolous and fanciful examples of work-making projects. The projects needed today must not only satisfy a quantitative requirement, but help bring about a qualitative transformation. While being kept sound and healthy, the Keynesian subsystem must be gradually diverted from an ever more epic output of bottles and cans to an increasing emphasis on personal services.

This is not likely to be an easy assignment. We shall, however, be able to enlist some unlikely allies for the task. The intimidating nature of our problem derives in part from the way in which mass media advertising tailors the tastes and the souls of the public. Our advertising talent must be seen as technicians with skills for packaging messages in a way that makes them accessible to the broad masses. The messages in themselves need not be meretricious. When economists have straightened out their thinking on economic matters, we shall have need of the advertising community to educate the public in the new economic rationale. With their aid it should be possible to reorientate our economy.[6]

6 It is notable with what frequency the need for a revision of our code of values is being expressed in the most contrasted areas of society. Thus F. Banks,

Of course, such a reorientation will inevitably have an effect on our price level, and could thus seriously upset our foreign trade balance. That is why it is important for international arrangements to be reached to permit the filtering out from export prices taxation that is related to essentially domestic services. Only in that way would countries acquire enough economic sovereignty to allow them to come to grips with their major problems. I shall examine this question in the next chapter.

I have traced some of the consequences of our economic pluralism, and the means of dealing with these. But with time that pluralism is likely to take on deeper significance. From a pluralistic pursuit of greater shares in the distribution of material goods, it will develop into a pluralism of values, a symbiosis of different life styles. More than a premonition of this has already appeared in the counter-culture of our rebel youth, seeking – at times in odd ways – values that our society has neglected. Up to now this has been expressed by confrontation, in the absolute polarization of good and evil. However, we are moving towards a more mature consideration of such issues.

The counter-culture is no longer viewed as simply a massive movement of desertion and 'copping out'. The rebels are even coming to be seen as having something to offer a society that is increasingly corralled in its own blind alley. The dissenter and even the eccentric social critic can be regarded as society's reserve of genetic materials – a store of alternatives to the established codes. As such they are not highly prized in normal periods; but they can acquire importance in time of crisis. That is all the more so when their warnings come to be increasingly confirmed by sober economic indices.

A vision is starting to take shape that it is perfectly feasible for a section of our population to turn their backs upon the acquisitive consumer society, and organize their lives by quite different principles. In fact, by doing so they might even be helping society make those adjustments that ecology and the rules of arithmetic are bidding us to make.

A promising version of this approach is offered by Arnold Simoni

---

whose specialty is the economics of minerals, writes: 'As for the industrial countries the long-run answer to the problems of mineral supply is probably going to involve an extensive alteration of consumption patterns, with sport and culture – to include education – playing a much larger part in the scheme of things.' *Problems of Mineral Supply* in *Future Resources and World Development* Plenum Press, New York and London, 1976, p. 74.

in an unpublished manuscript.[7]

'Basically, we should give to every person enough money for shelter and food. Everyone, without exception, should receive this money, and there the obligation of society for the individual's welfare would end. Any money the individual makes above this minimum is his; the minimum payment is not reduced.

'This means that the basic security of each individual would be assured, and each would choose how much work, and of what sort, he or she wanted to do to supplement it. Many would be willing to trade a higher standard of living for greater leisure, and this would be fine – indeed, it would be encouraged. Others would do only the amount of work that suited them, and would find the level that they wanted. Those with interesting, vital and satisfying jobs would stay in them, while others would have the security to look around for such jobs for themselves.

'There would be no social stigma attached to receiving the minimum income, because it would come to everyone. In addition, the need to conserve resources would put conspicuous consumption under a cloud, and make it acceptable to live economically. As consumer commodities go up in price, with the rise in the cost of the energy and the resources needed to make them, the net gain to be achieved by an expansion of income will reduced, and it will make sense to more and more people to be content with basic necessities. . . .

'It is a commonplace in discussions of minimum income schemes that it would be cheaper to pay everyone a minimum income, than to pay for the bureaucracy necessary to administer the present welfare system. The principal objection to it is usually based on fears that it will reduce the incentive to work. Since that is our objective, however, what is seen as a liability through Third Age eyes becomes an asset. The Third Age is based on insecurity – "work or starve" – and consequently welfare has been made to seem like a shameful thing. In the Fourth Age, however, it must be accepted that society has an obligation to provide a minimum level of security to all its citizens, and that all citizens have a responsibility to limit their consumption of resources to a level that the enviroment can sustain. . . .

'The minimum income plan would allow the entire welfare system to be dismantled, as well as unemployment insurance administration and employment departments.'

---

7 *Time Frame – The Fourth Age of Man.* p. 203.

Simoni's plan conforms to the modular congruence calculus explained in this book. The basic income is not taxed or taken into account in assessing taxation on any additional earnings. This serves to withdraw important layers of social lien from price, and to restore viability to entire areas of the private sector. It reduces the needless return-trip transfers between the public and private sectors that add to the dead weight of bureaucracy and disturb the patterns of price.

To reap the full implications of this, however, Simoni's scheme can be carried further: with it there is no need for a high minimum wage, or possibly for any minimum wage at all. Much of the protection that workers get from minimum wage should be available from the basic income. In combination with this, an unrestricted market wage would be more advantageous to the worker because the basic income would not be taxable or considered in the tax liability of other earnings. He would have enough income to protect him against grosser exploitation. On the other hand, with lower minimum wages or no minimum wage at all, we would reduce the threshold of economic feasibility that determines what work gets done and whom it is economic to employ. At present much important work remains undone because there is no way of assimilating it into our accountancy.[8]

For centuries humanity has had its dreams of a golden age of leisure. And then when the marvels of technology seemed about to put leisure within our grasp, we have had it snatched away by entropy accumulations in our society. To prevent this we must take time out and devise ways of getting around these.

---

8 Minimum wages legislation, a praiseworthy thing in its original context, is coming in for a growing volume of criticism as contributing to the hopeless lot of the unskilled, chronically unemployed. Thus *Time* (August 29th, 1977) quotes David Reisman to the effect that the minimum wage is the 'product of an alliance of the better situated labor union with the liberals against the deprived and the elderly, whom people would otherwise employ for household or city work that doesn't get done.'

Chapter Seven

The Imperialism of Bad Price Theory

An entire literature exists on the deterioration of the terms of trade of the underdeveloped countries in their dealings with the industrialized nations.[1] And yet, for lack of an adequate price theory, possibly the most important factor contributing to this has been overlooked.

The disadvantage of raw material producers on the markets of the world does not arise only from their lack of market power. It has its roots, too, in the very different incidence of the Social Lien – the taxation layer in price – in the goods that the Third World exports and in those that it buys from the advanced lands.

The industrial commodities that it imports are end-products of a many-tiered production sequence. At each stage of this, taxation is injected into costs. This does not add to price in just a linear way. The accretions of taxation are compounded: taxation is levied on the taxation already levied at the earlier links.

The exports of the underdeveloped country, however, have a very distinct price structure. For the most part they consist of raw materials, or lightly processed goods. The ladder of their productive process has a single or at most very few rungs: there are fewer occasions for taxation to enter price. Moreover, the tax rates will reflect the precarious

1 'Indeed according to one UNCTAD estimate, by 1972 "the terms of trade of these countries had deteriorated by about 15 per cent, compared with the mid-1950's, equivalent to a loss, in 1972 of about $10,000 million, or rather more than 20 per cent of these countries' aggregate exports, and considerably exceeding the total of official development assistance from developed market economy countries to developing countries in Africa, Asia, and Latin America (some $8,400 million in 1972)." In other words there was, in effect, a net transfer of real resources, over this period, from developing to developed countries, the flow of aid being more than offset by the adverse trend in the developing countries.' Paul Rogers, editor, *Future Resources and World Development*, Plenum Press, New York and London. 1976, p. 50.

physical infrastructures and sketchy social services in these countries. For these things are important determinants of the amount of social lien in price.

On the other hand the prices of their imports will be part-payment for the costly social services of the advanced societies.

Viewed in the prespective of the present book, it is clear that the underveloped lands are being burdened with part of the costs of public services abroad that their citizens have no access to. For their part, the industrial countries profit in their import prices by the sparse provision of such services in backward lands. From this there results a major break-down in elementary distributory justice. Economists have borne witness to the consequences, but have not suspected the cause. It is as a rule attributed to the different degrees of market power of these countries (which is a contributing factor), and to the machinations of the former imperialist powers. It has not occurred to many that it may be also due to the simple failure of economic theory – everybody's economic theory, that of the ex-colonials and that of the ex-colonists.

Unwittingly, the developed countries have been levying an onerous tribute upon the underdeveloped ones, a tribute many times as great as the token aid that they have extended to them.

Nor does the matter end there. To defend themselves against what they sense intuitively to be a massive aggression by the advanced economies, the Third World lands strike out blindly with programs that would only compound the harm done by our wrong-headed price theory, if they could be realized. And, of course, occasionally they can be realized. Oil is a case in point.

As early as 1968, the Sixteenth O.P.E.C. conference called for posted petroleum prices that 'would move in such a manner as to prevent any deterioration in their relationship to the prices of manufactured goods traded internationally.'[2] The raw material producers thus try catching up in a single-tiered productive process with the taxation injected into price in the course of a whole succession of operations that go into making finished industrial goods. The balance of this model is readily constructed.

The higher raw material and energy costs created by this mirroring of the social lien in the price of the industrial exports adds new layers to price in the industrial lands. We have not only the original social lien

2 Philip Connelly and Robert Perlman, *The Politics of Scarcity, Resource Conflicts,* Oxford University Press, London, New York and Toronto, 1975, p. 132. Paul Rogers, editor.

in their price structure, but its echo bounced off the prices of Third World exports. And, of course, the process does not stop there; the social lien is thus transformed into an infinite non-convergent series.

Up to now this has occurred only in the case of petroleum and a few raw materials such as coffee and cacao where market relationships suddenly placed power in the hands of the producer countries. But as soon as a favorable situation crops up, this pattern cannot fail to recur. And when raw-material producing lands are not able to implement such programs, their frustration is all the greater. For in that case they are the helpless victims not only of prices burdened by needless social lien in the price of their industrial imports, but of the successful riposte of those primary producers who have the power to defend themselves.

A basic accounting error foisted upon us by economic theory has thus been stripping these lands of a good part of the scant capital that they need for their development and survival. In dollars and cents this has redounded to the advantage of the powerful economies, but it has transferred an alien entropy build-up to a sector of the international system that can ill support it. This threatens the breakdown of the whole system.

Here again, modular congruence calculus helps establish the extent of the resulting damage – assessing the number of times that the original misplaced social lien in the price of the industrial exports turns up in echo-effect in further transactions. By the principle of this calculus two wrongs do not cancel out to make a right, but merely escalate the disruption. Our international price structure has been violently disfigured through misdirected impositions of social lien where it does not belong, and by the reprisals brought on by it.

Nor does the matter end there.

In a great part of the underdeveloped world processes of social revalorization are at work no less than in the industrialized lands. Deep-going reassessments of social orderings and income distribution are underway that have nothing to do with purely market forces. But these processes can be inflamed by our inequitable international price structure.

Under the heading of social revalorization in the Third World, some very different phenomena occur. To illustrate the point I can do no better than quote from an excellent essay of F. E. Banks:

'In the discussion of equity between producer and consumer that constitutes a large part of the so-called "works program" of the United Nations, and to a certain extent the CIPEC secretariat, it must be remembered that the rate of profit never comes into consideration, only the movement of prices. However, given the fact that the wages in South America and Africa are at most one-third of those in North America and Canada, and that seams are much richer, it is possible to argue that profit rates are high by an international measure – although not high enough to compensate for the low productivity of the rest of the economy. This, of course, is the crux of the matter.

'The underdeveloped countries producing copper want a price which while it will not allow workers and technicians in this industry to enjoy a standard of living in the vicinity of their co-workers in the industrial countries – will enable diverse functionaries, officials, and the like, *outside* the industry to maintain themselves in a fashion completely incommensurate with the contribution they are prepared to make to the economies of their respective countries. Under the circumstances it can be submitted that no price, regardless of how high it is, would suffice. It can also be submitted that this situation prevails in most underdeveloped countries, and is relevant for the entire range of primary commodities.'[3]

The nationalization of much of the raw material production in underdeveloped countries in recent years has a bearing on all this. It has in effect transferred many of the determinants of production and pricing from one entropy system to another.

Let me quote Banks once more: 'Prior to the early 1960's, the history of copper prices and the future of copper was mostly a matter of concern for the directors and stockholders of the large copper-producing companies. . . All this was changed by the nationalisation of many of the copper companies that began in the 1960's. Prior to these nationalisations the burden of a collapse in the price of this or that raw material fell on the firm producing it. With the nationalisations this burden was transferred to the countries in which this producing capacity was located.'[4]

The output and pricing of a raw material export may thus come to answer logics unrelated to those of the market or the need to conserve non-renewable resources. The rationale that takes over may be one or more of the following: 1) the acquisition of resources to support an ambitious development policy; 2) the acquisition of foreign exchange to sustain such a policy; 3)the earning of the foreign exchange to support the native political elite in a style comparable to that of the upper and

3 op. cit. p. 68. Paul Rogers, editor.
4 op. cit. p. 66. Paul Rogers, editor.

middle classes of the developed lands.

In listing such non-market rationales, value judgments are irrelevant to our purpose. Once you grant the premises, the conclusions of any of these systems follow with an impeccable consistency. What is important is that their logics are not those of the market.

In its own way, each embodies an essay in social revalorization. For example, in 1) and 2) the guiding sociological model may call for the bringing to the backward country of patterns of production *and distribution* closer to those prevailing in the industrialized lands. In 3) the model for a production pattern possibly more like that of the advanced countries, but there is no intention of imitating their distribution patterns. In a sense it identifies the interests of the poor country with those of their upper social strata, and it is the consumption of these that are to be brought to or maintained at the levels of the wealthy countries. Goals of military prestige or territorial aggrandizement may also enter into one or more of these models.

Of course, the logic in question cannot be imposed upon the market from without unless its advocates exercise sufficient political power; or, as in the case of the oil-producing lands in 1973, unless their market power is so overwhelming that they can impose their political rationale upon the market.

Clearly it is necessary to seek a way of defusing this explosive chain. Unless a common denominator is found to these contrasted logics, we must inevitably end up with futile confrontation rather than with a coherent policy. This was illustrated by the proceedings of the Stockholm Conference on the Human Environment of June, 1972. Much to the fore in the minds of the delegates was the booklet *Limits to Growth,* summarizing the well-known study of Forrester and Meadows for the Club of Rome. But rather than dealing significantly with the problems analysed in it, the Conference was taken up largely with confrontations of the respective power groups.[5]

And yet certain bed-rock facts remain. Even allowing for technological revolutions, it is doubtful that our non-renewable resources will allow the continued exponential growth of the mass-production industries in the advanced countries. It is quite certain that they will

5 op. cit., Robert Dickson and Paul Rogers, *Resources, Producer Power and International Relations:* 'It may well be that for all its concerns with the problems of the industrial nations, the Stockholm conference will go down in history as the forum which provided a major impetus for the notion of producer power.'

not permit the degree of industrialization attained in these lands to be reproduced in the underdeveloped countries; most certainly not when we include the exponential growth pattern inherent in that set-up. Redistribute the resources and raw material reserves? That is a reasonable enough program, but it cannot be seriously broached unless it is complemented with another. A high degree of industrialization implies appropriate human capital and institutions. That in turn requires that the rate of population growth be brought into alignment with the resources available for the necessary education, health and social policies.

The refashioning of values and life styles involved in this is nothing that can be limited to the Third World.

There are other negentropies that the advanced countries must seek in the Third World apart from raw materials. We have seen that they are pressing upon their reserves of workers prepared to do manual and menial jobs. Their needs in this respect have been filled by immigration, legal and illegal, permanent and temporary. At best, however, this is a stop-gap in dealing with entropy build-up. The immigrants and their offspring inevitably assimilate to the standards of the host country, and contribute to reproduce the problem on an expanded scale.

There is then a need for exploring alternative or complementary ways of tapping the potential differences between the labor conditions of the advanced and underdeveloped countries. Part of the solution would be to concentrate more of the world's labor-intensive industries in countries with an excess of such labor, and its capital-intensive industries in the highly industrialized lands. Undoubtedly, any such proposal will be denounced as an imperialist conspiracy to keep the Third World dependent upon the industrial powers. However, a sober reading of the resources and energy prospects of the world casts serious doubt that the present pattern of industrialization can even be continued where it exists, let alone copied in the backward portions of the world. Moreover, the unemployment situations in these weak, young economies are clamoring for attention. What capital is available should be spread to afford a maximum opportunity for as many of the people as possible.[6]

---

6 Adapting one's culture to the resources available is by no means the same as downgrading it. Even a cultural achievement of the order of China's cuisine reflects the ecological constraints amongst which it developed: its use of meats is sparing, and of dairy products nil. With its population density China could not afford the extensive soil exploitation implied in a meat diet. Yet who would be bold enough to argue that this was a handicap to China's gourmets?

Essential to any such arrangement would be the willingness of the advanced countries to keep their markets open to such labor-intensive imports.

There are many possibilities in this direction that could be explored. For example, the costliness of labor in the advanced countries has led to the practice of scrapping rather than repairing many sub-assemblies of mass-produced products. This involves a waste of materials and energy. If local labor costs make the repairing of such assemblies impractical, it might in some cases be possible for the manufacturers to arrange for them to be sent to plants in underdeveloped countries for rebuilding. In many of these lands, where skilled labor is cheap, automobiles are kept running for decades after their contemporaries have ended up on the scrap heap in North America. The structures of multi-national corporations might prove of use in organizing such interchange.

Obviously such plans call for wide-ranging international agreements. In these the following policy operators would be of central importance:

1) Rebates of certain types of taxation on exports would be permitted and encouraged. This would not only ease the burden on the Third World and correct the terms of international trade; it would open up the possibilities of much-needed capital accumulation to help these countries restructure their economies. Such an arrangement would extend the detaxation techniques outlined in our previous chapter to international trade, where their scope is even greater than domestically.

2) International arrangements to locate labor-intensive industries in the under-developed lands, in return for the abandonment of uneconomic projects for capital-intensive industries in such countries. This would both lessen the entropy build-up connected with the cost and availability of unskilled and semi-skilled labor in the advanced economies and provide employment in the Third World. The overall effect on the international price level would also be helpful.

3) A recognition of the structural price gradient would highlight the key importance of long-term credits (at less than market rates) for the development of the Third World. Predictably much of the real principal of such loans would be eroded before maturity. In return for such loans, it would only be fair for the industrialized countries to be assured concerning their raw material supplies at relatively stable prices. It would thus be feasible to restrict the price movement of such commodities to cost increases (including higher wages actually paid the workers producing them) plus a factor reflecting the depletion of non-renewable resources. In this way the industrialized world would be

protected against the prices on raw material markets being distorted by political power plays.

The taxbond technique could be applied to multi-national corporations operating in underdeveloped countries. Both the host country and the country of origin could offer tax exemptions if a portion of taxable income were made available to the developing country.

Clearly in all these areas enough elbowroom will remain for bargaining between the negotiating parties. However, focussed in this way in terms of the basic logics and restraints of our reality, this approach could lead to solutions that would serve the interests of all sides. In the long run, our present blind confrontations can be helpful to no one.

The importance of filtering out the tax-cost of domestic public services from world prices is not only of concern to the Third World. It is also taking on importance for countries at the other end of the spectrum of development.

In a general way such development follows a definite pattern: first comes the transition from pre-capitalist work forms to labor-intensive industries; then emphasis shifts from labor-intensive industries to physical capital-intensive ones, such as iron and steel and engineering. Finally a trend makes itself felt from enterprises intensive in physical capital to those based on a high investment in human capital – towards what might be described as a post-industrial society. In the latter the output of personal services takes primacy over the mass production of commodities. Not only are personal services of a highly evolved type required to develop the indicated technologies and personnel, but the citizens of such a society necessarily demand and have need of a higher quality of life. All this implies a growing investment by the state in education and other personal services that our current public accountancy does not even recognize as an investment. This results in a needless burden of social lien in the price of exports. For example, it is certainly an important if completely neglected factor in the poor performance of Great Britain on the world market.

No matter how obsolescent her industrial plant may be, or how crippling some of her trade union regulations, the fact is that Britain continues as the repository of a considerable portion of humanity's intellectual achievements. This finds expression not only in the quality of much of her educational system and culture, but in the position that she still occupies in certain of the frontiers of science.[7] Indeed,

7 For example, Britain's export of superb television productions stands in significant contrast to her record in engineering exports.

part of Britain's export difficulties are not unrelated to the high cost of all this. For under existing arrangements the tax burden for the support of this intellectual achievement weighs heavily upon its export price structure.

It would be a great loss both for Britain and the world, if misconceived compulsions of price stabilization and false economy were to induce her government to allow the deterioration of its scientific and intellectual life. If the problem were viewed in the perspective of a relevant economic theory, this need not occur. Investment in human capital could be treated as investment and fittingly amortized to lessen the corresponding tax-burden on price. And personal services not directly related to the production of exports would be treated as strictly domestic items: their tax-cost would not be allowed to encumber export prices. Clearly, however, the rebating of such taxes would have to be negotiated by international agreement.

Nor is this a problem peculiar to Britain. The same factor is showing up in the commercial relations of the United States and Japan. The current sweep of the American market by Japanese steel and automobiles is not to be explained entirely by the more modern and efficient nature of some of the Japanese industries involved, or by the Japanese expertise in the design and production of small cars. It is not even to be accounted for entirely by the unique social disciplines inherited from pre-Meiji Japan. Part of the American disadvantage in this encounter is related to the very pre-eminence of the United States in areas based on an intensive use of human capital. Prominent amongst these, of course, are those having to do with technological and scientific frontiers. An economy that can import much of its basic technology will at a certain point enjoy an advantage in the export of mass-produced products based on the heavy investment of physical capital; for its price structure will not be burdened by the elaborate investment in human capital and personal services needed for the development of these technologies.

It is not difficult to foresee a time when Japan itself come under the pressure from export competition of other countries who can concentrate on physical capital-intensive industries with less investment in human capital than Japan has been making.

We must learn to free our international price structure from a needless overburden of social lien. If we fail to do so, humanity will be unable to rise above the role of compulsive mass producers of commodities; we shall in fact undermine its ability to turn out even the commodities that it really needs. Only when we have unscrambled the cost of purely domestic services from our export prices, will we acquire some control over the style and quality of the lives we lead. Only then shall our society cease being an adjunct of a malfunctioning industrial machine.

Chapter Eight

War-Paint and Economic Cannibalism

The more complex the configuration, the greater the variety of patterns that will appear as we alter the angle of our vision. Not only may we miss seeing the forest before us, but, depending upon where we stand, different trees will obstruct our view.

In this book, I have dealt essentially with the mandatory arithmetic imposed by the circuits of our mixed economy. Where alternatives really exist, I have made a point of leaving open the choice of goals. My concern was to bring to the fore the 'full costing' of public services, and the inevitable effects of the structural changes in our economy on its entropy systems. Only with a knowledge of such factors will we be in a position to make rational decisions.

The time has now come to look at our forest in another perspective. I will consider the consequences if we go on seeing only the tree before our nose.

For a useful point of departure we can turn to the sociologists. That discipline has drawn attention to the gap that can separate 'manifest' and 'latent' function, the difference between the apparent motive of social behavior and its deeper roots.[1] Georges Gurvitch, in particular, developed this concept. He saw social phenomena taking place on many different levels of reality. The logics operating on these levels are addressed to different needs; like lines on parallel planes these may not meet. Gurvitch lists some of these levels: the ecological context, the social models including collective signs and signals, the organized apparatus, the social roles, the social symbols.

1 Robert K. Merton, *Social Theory and Social Structure,* The Free Press, N.Y., 1965, p. 62. *Traité de Sociologie publié sous la direction de Georges Gurvitch,* T. 1, Presses Universitaires de France, 1967, p. 158 et seq.

'By social symbols we understand signs that express only part of the content signified. These serve as bridges between the content and the collective and individual agents to whom they are directed. Every symbol has two poles; on the one hand it is an incomplete sign, an inadequate expression; on the other it is an instrument of participation.'

By playing upon our emotions, symbols can by-pass the circuits of reason, and reconcile opposites. There are times when this is helpful for social cohesion. Though in their origins a useful device, they can come to do us a disservice if we become locked in the symbols of a dead period.

Much of the debate on economic issues in our day takes place on such different levels of reality.

In part this reflects the fact that the division of labor has led to an extreme fragmentation of reality. Even within a single discipline the mass of knowledge has grown too vast for any one mind. In the physical sciences the tests for the other fellow holding up his end of this division of labor are as a rule clear and decisive: the bomb explodes or is a dud; the astronaut gets to the moon or doesn't. In the social sciences, however, we must assume that those who labor in the other specialties know what they are doing. And the broad public even more so. Basically the whole structure is cemented by faith reinforced by the discipline of a priesthood.

There are, of course, those who do attempt to audit the whole, and to raise disturbing questions of scientific method. Increasingly, however, their role has come to resemble that of God's fools in the Dark Ages.

Consider for a moment what they are up against. There is, to begin with, the antinomy between the mass culture of a pluralistic society and the elitist nature of science. For the politician, that grand mediator who holds the purse-strings, even the relative truths that we can hope to attain in the social sciences could prove a cumbersome asset. What are useful to him are chips and flakings from it, shaped to fit the slots of political process. Technological and social revolutions are making unprecedented demands on society's power of adaptation; but its ability to adjust to these has become dangerously sapped.

In an age of communications virtuosity, we have become powerless to communicate on many issues that really matter. The different social groups find themselves talking at the top of their voices on different wave-lengths about different things in different tongues under the illusion that they are carrying on a dialogue.

With some groups the argument serves as catharsis, for others it may be an exercise in nostalgia. Yet others will be taking part in an ideological fashion parade. The politician may be mounting a ladder to office. Labor and capital will often be fighting the battles of a generation or two ago, vying with each other in misreading the messages of today's prices. About the only thing that the contestants will share is a lack of curiosity about the real effect of whatever they are proposing on the economy as a whole.

Gurvitch places great stress on the variety of time horizons in which we do our thinking.[2] There are societies that do most of their thinking in forward time; others have a retrospective time orientation. Periods of upheaval and restructuring are likely to show a 'time of irregular beat. . . .'

The scientific achievements of the past three centuries left us leaning heavily upon our future and paying little heed to our past. One aspect of this is our readiness to believe that we can seize that future in a single mathematical formula, like a lepidopterist does a butterfly. From a many-to-many correspondence of inexhaustable richness and possibility, the relationship between the present and the future has been stripped to an impoverished one-to-one model. Marc Bloch remarked that by immersing ourselves in our past we grow 'antennae' invaluable for society's orientation and survival. Conventional theory has deprived us of these antennae.

Inevitably, a reaction has set in. From an impatience with our past, we are recoiling in horror from the future that we have created for ourselves. But some of the forms assumed by this reversal have an unmistakable anti-social note.

Gurvitch sees 'times of uncertainty to be par excellence associated with "illusory time" *(trompe l'oeil).'* This is the time-dimension of the costume ball. Thus the Hapsburgs before Napoleon acted out the Holy Roman Empire; Napoleon III the role of his uncle. But there is no need to delve into history for instances of such 'illusory time'. Our own age, through the failure of our economic theory, is rummaging the attics of the past for plausible plots.

That search is not a strenuous one. A convincing villain practically brings his plot with him. And the promise of price stability made by conventional economic theory can lead only to one conclusion: there must be monumental villainy afoot.

Recrimination has become the common coin of economic inter-

---

2 Gurvitch, op. cit. p. 164.

course. And increasingly there are suggestions of deeper, unavowed meanings to some of our most gleaming crusades. Population pressure have increased in our cities, and that has never made for tolerance in human relations. Fernand Braudel, for example, has explained the religious wars and persecutions that swept 16th-century Europe by the outstripping of food resources by population. There is no reason to assume that the gulf between declared motives and effective causes have narrowed in our day.[3]

What we are witnessing is the threatening dissolution of our economic system into a network of zero-sum games. Whenever any group runs headlong into an objective constraint – say the arithmetical tables – its first impulse is to make an opponent responsible for its disappointment. There are, of course, real zero-sum game situations in our economy; but to identify them would call for a sophisticated understanding of that economy. When society, however, comes up against an objective constraint, what we have is not a zero-sum game (though the deck-chairs can be rearranged on the sinking Titanic), but a game in which all parties can be losers. Such a scenario, though closer to the truth, is less useful on political platforms.

The zero-sum scenario, however, becomes plausible only if reality is hidden by an appropriate screen theory. The sinister potential of such screen theories is unlimited. Ours is not the first case of a society that started devouring its accumulated reserves when it found its ability to produce impaired. In the Dark Ages the monuments of the ancient world were used as stone quarries. And as they were being torn down, the true nature of the operation was undoubtedly masked by a satisfying screen theory: the sinful pagan temples were being razed for Christian ends.

If we scan the contemporary economic scene with an eye to real

---

3 'The proof of the overpopulation of Mediterranean Europe of the period, were it needed, can be seen in the repeated expulsion of the Jews. They are driven out of Castille and in 1597 out of Portugal. . . . Is it bold to maintain . . . that in countries with too great a population for their resources . . . religion is the pretext as much as the cause of persecution and emigration? Similarly at a later dates the law of numbers will come into effect against the Moors in the Spain of Philip III, and much later, this time in France . . . against the Protestants under Louis XIV'. Fernand Braudel, *La Mediterranée et le Monde Mediterranéen à l'époque de Philippe II* – Librairie Armand Colin, Paris, 1949, p.357.

Jewish refugees from Spain, along with many Christian deserters, were received in the more sparsely populated Turkish domains with open arms.

significance rather than proclaimed intents, only one conclusion is possible: our society has begun cannibalizing its economy. The phenomenon is turning up in the most diverse areas. It is rooted in the attempt to take more out of that economy than is being put into it – an exercise abetted by our economic theory.

The same government that gives priority of the 'fight against inflation' is likely to be living substantially on the avails of the price gradient. That lifts nominal earnings into higher tax brackets; and through the astigmatism of equilibrium theory, the increase in the replacement cost of fixed capital and inventory is seen as taxable earnings. If by some miracle prices were stabilized, there are few governments in the Western world who would not find themselves in heavy trouble.

It is many years now that some accountants have advocated LIFO ('Last In First Out') as a more realistic way of calculating inventory values. Taking the historical rather than the replacement costs of inventory means eating into the capital needed by firms to function. When LIFO was first proposed there was no question of a structural price gradient having become a standing feature of the economy. It is all the more necessary today: what was a random injustice at the time has become a systematic encroachment upon the capital of businesses.

LIFO, however, would still leave the greater problem of fixed capital unresolved. Because of the longer life of fixed capital as compared with that of inventories, the damage resulting from tax-collectors ignoring the price gradient is all the greater. Accountants have been warning of the liquidity crisis that is shaping as a result of this.[4]

As we have noted, one of the important trends of our times has been the shift of the gravity center of society's accumulation from the private to the public sector, and from physical to human capital. By pretending that the price gradient does not exist, governments grossly over-value the profits of the private sector; at the same time they shut their eyes to the existence of much public investment in both human capital and finance it out of current revenue. On both counts they needlessly increase the burden of taxation on the private firm, and in a way that is especially destructive of its negentropy.

I am less concerned here with the justice of the performance than with the circumstance that it cannot possibly work. That governments

---

4 Economic Council of Canada, *Thirteenth Annual Review. The inflation Dilemma,* Minister of Supply and Services, Ottawa, 1976, pp. 64.

should imagine that they can get away with such an operation for very long, indicates the decay of economic understanding in our day.

There are many other ways in which the state cannibalizes the private sector. The investor who sells shares of stocks after having held them for many years, pays taxes on his nominal profit, though the real values of the proceeds of his sale may be far below his purchase price. What is objectionable in such dodges is not that the revenue in question accrues to the state: it may be that for its good works the state has need of it. It is rather the unconscionable, self-defeating way in which it is collected.

An intelligent dairy farmer, no matter what the edge of his appetite, will be concerned with the well-being of his herd. He knows that if he barbecues his cows, he will very soon be out of the dairy business. Governments have not always attained such wisdom.

It is not the state alone that is preying upon the economy. The struggle for shares of the national income has degenerated into predatory inroads on the capital stock essential for the maintenance of the national income.

The classical example, of course, is rent controls. The contra-productive effects of rent controls in bringing about a decline in the rental housing stock have been commented upon by economists of the most diverse schools. Indeed, anyone unfamiliar with the mechanics of political decision might marvel that the issue should have become an actual one again.[5] Consider, however, how irresistible its lures. The

5 *Rent Control, A Popular Paradox, Evidence of the Economic Effects of Rent Control,* Fraser Institute, Vancouver, 1975, contains essays by economists ranging from Hayek and Milton Friedman to Sven Rydenfeldt summing up the experience of Sweden's Socialist government in the field.

Rent Review was introduced in the Province of Ontario in August, 1975. In Toronto, twenty-five percent of gross rents go to pay municipal taxes. Because this is paid ostensibly by landlords rather than tenants, assessments are distorted to average 26.5 percent of market price in the case of rental housing as compared to 8.7 percent in the case of owner-occupied housing. The stabilization policies of the Bank of Canada drove first mortgage rates to over 12 percent in 1975, the year Rent Review was introduced — an increase of some fifty percent in six years. Mortgage interest payments make up about fifty percent of gross rents, so that the increase in the interest rate alone account for about one quarter of the increase in gross rents over that period.

Rent Review in Ontario allows the landlord no return on his investment if he did not earn such a return before Rent Review was introduced. This strikes at the heart of an industry that traditionally has operated much of the time less for current profits than in the hope of developing such in the future.

screen theory that goes with it is particularly persuasive: an increasing number of the tenants in our large cities cannot afford rents, even though they may reflect the landlord's costs. An alien logic thus replaces the constraints of accountancy: the landlord's costs and solvency are ruled to be his private affair. The point is that the landlord makes a superb political target, and the taxation system in many countries have exploited this to the hilt. In effect tenants have been invited to consume the rental housing stock as though it were a hot-dog at a political picnic.

Whatever the merits of price controls in our mixed economy, one thing is clear: there is no possibility of a useful program of price controls unless you have some idea of what norm you are controlling prices to. This in turn calls for an economic theory relevant to our realities. In the absence of that, price controls must rest on the premise that prices have been dislocated and have to be reset like a broken leg. However, profound and irreversible structural forces have been at work in our price movement – quite apart from any genuinely inflationary factors

---

Though capital repairs are amortized, the interest on the unamortized portion of such expenditures is disallowed by Rent Review as a cost in determining rents. The same government, however, levies a capital tax on all borrowings of incorporated companies – including those for such capital repairs by landlords. That tax increased by 200 percent between 1973 and 1977 – from .1 to .3 percent of the amount of the borrowings. This is a perfect example of a bureaucracy trying to summon something out of the void, of finally discovering perpetual motion.

The broadest discretionary powers are given to an improvised civil service so that the government can achieve the desired political statistic without shouldering responsibility for the logic whereby it is attained.

Above all, there is no attempt to coordinate the guidlines governing Rent Review with certain elementary facts concerning housing costs that should be known to that same government from its public housing arm, the Ontario Housing Corporation. In 1977 Ontario Housing Corporation projects in Metro Toronto ran up an operating loss of 81 million dollars; this required a Government subsidy of $240.72 per month for each of the 28,168 housing units concerned. Significantly this figure exceeded the *total average rent disallowed private landlords by Rent Review* during this same period. This statistic received no comment from legislators or editorialists.

More recently to try overcoming the complete stoppage in the construction of private rental housing, the federal and provincial governments have announced heavy subsidies to builders of rental housing. By the modular congruence calculus introduced in this book, the contra-productive nature of all this policy is apparent.

Rent Review Provisional Landlord's Guide to Cost Revenue Statement, Ontario, Ministry of Consumer and Commercial Relations, 1976; Toronto *Globe and Mail,* November 5th, 1977.

that may exist at certain times. These make the simplistic bone-setting notion contraproductive. In applying it, governments have played havoc with the negentropies of the private sector.[6]

As so often happens, the phenomenon of economic cannibalism has received its crowning expression on the stock market. With the prospects of the private sector beclouded and the risks surrounding it multiplied, the stock market has developed a catatonic way of ignoring improved company earnings even when they do occur. At the same time the continued climb of prices has opened an ever-widening gap between share prices and the value of the physical assets of the given company – another negentropy, if you please. This invites still another form of economic cannibalism – the company take-over. An increasingly high proportion of the dramatic leaps of share prices on a sagging market is associated with such take-overs. The company acquiring control simply ingests the grossly undervalued assets of the company.

Another variant of the same scenario is for the company management to gobble up the major part of the other shareholders' equity by acquiring their shares at the market price, and then 'going private'. In this way they are often able to buy up the shares at a small fraction of the price at which they were issued years earlier. What has been ailing the market quotation in many case has not been the company's condition (which management, of course, would know best), but the state of the world at large. And by going private, management may not only profit by the anxiety-ridden appraisals of the stock market, but disentangle their company from its further syndromes.

Our thinking on economic matters is threatened with disintegration into parochial fragments. On every side we find groups acting out their own particular scenario in illusory time. And all this comes when the realities of our pluralistic economy are imposing the need for a complex and highly disciplined time-structure on our thinking. The price gradient makes it necessary for us to do our planning in terms of temporal cost zones. To obstruct a necessary project so that it is shifted from one temporal cost zone to another can be damaging, even ruinous to society. We have intimidating time-leads to meet. For it is a characteristic of exponential development that it sneaks up upon the unprepared like a thief in the night. In such a setting the tolerances for delay and

6 Thus the Anti-Inflation Board in Canada, introduced in 1975, puts a ceiling on the profits from a firm's entire operations during the year. If the profits on all items produced exceed this ceiling in the early part of the year, corresponding losses must be incurred during the rest of the period to restore the balance.

error becomes paper thin. We simply cannot afford much play-acting in illusory time. No matter how large the audience, and enthusiastic the claque, such productions are bound to have a short run.[7]

Jay W. Forrester has written that 'the human mind is not adapated to interpreting how social systems behave. Our social systems belong to the class called multiple-loop non-linear feedback systems. In the long history of human evolution it has not been necessary for man to understand these systems until very recent historical times. Evolutionary processes have not given us the mental skill needed to interpret properly the dynamic behavior of the systems of which we have now become a part.

'In addition, the social sciences have fallen into some mistaken "scientific" practices that compound man's natural shortcomings. Computers are often used for what the computer does poorly and the human mind does well. At the same time the human mind is used for what the human mind does poorly and the computer does well. Even worse, impossible tasks are attempted while achievable and important goals are ignored.' [8]

The physical subsystems of our complex urbanized world have a structure that is similar to that of our economic subsystems. In them there are the same feedbacks and non-linear relationships. Moreover, the physical and economic systems intermesh as parts of a still more embracing system. Thinking in terms of abstract structure is the basis for group theory and many other fertile branches of mathematics. There is no reason why the method should not be extended to the social sciences: it would at least allow a better intuitive grasp of our problems.

In the light of this, Roberto Vacca's views on the dangers of breakdown of our physical systems acquire importance.[9] He foresees a general collapse of our urban societies triggered by a chain of accidents, in which the blockage of one subsystem leads to the stalling of others. Thus a bottleneck of city traffic might initiate the chain reaction, in

---

7 The classic example developed by Meadows in the case of the water lillies in a pond that double the area already covered every so many days. Things seem tolerable right until it is too late to do very much about it: when the pond is only half covered it is one jump away from being completely smothered. Such are the surprises of exponential development.

8 *Counterintuitive Behavior of Social Systems,* in *Collected Papers of Jay W. Forrester,* Wright-Allen Press, Cambridge, Mass., 1975, p. 211.

9 *Demain le Moyen Age, La Dégradation des grands systèmes,* Paris, Albin Michel, 1973, p. 228.

the course of which neither the fire-fighters, doctors or the police, immobilized in the traffic jam, can intervene to put out a fire and prevent looting. Meanwhile the telephone system becomes overloaded and paralyzed owing to the volume of calls for aid. Since the teams of air traffic controllers cannot be replaced at the end of their shift because their relief is not able to get through the traffic jam, the controllers eventually succumb to fatigue. Sooner or later a plane will miss the runway and hit a high-tension line. This will knock out the power of an entire section of the city . . . and so on. The disaster escalates in tribute to the very intricacy of our technology. What is involved is a running down of the negentropy of reserves discussed in an earlier chapter.

We run the risk of falling victims to our partialization of reality under cover of screen theories. That such screen theories evoke high ethical principles merely underlines the need to redefine what ethics is about – what is social-minded and what is anti-social. From systems analysis we know that applying the logic of a single subsystem to a complex system is likely to be contraproductive. By this very fact the noble intent proclaimed in the screen premises of the exercise, is likely to be transmuted into its opposite.

A conclusion follows: any economic program that is advanced without an attempt to explore its effects on all subsystems, and thus its total cost, must be seen as anti-social. A project that attempts to deal with these things can be judged good or bad; one that does not even make the effort must be ruled out in advance as anti-social. This rule is tantamount to a simple lemma: the pluralism of our society cannot work without a pluralistic sense of responsibility.

Appendix

Vanishing Shelter

by Prof. Samuel Madras, Liberal Science Program,

Faculty of Science, York University.

Like so much else in our society, our housing situation seems to have reached a watershed in the mid-1960's, and, having done so, started on a downhill course. Before that, few people had questioned that our homes would go right on getting bigger and better – just as they had in the two decades after the war. Municipalities, developers, and government agencies had vied with one another in raising housing specifications – greater floor areas, larger lots, more elaborate servicing, more garage space, more plumbing and other extras. And then, without warning, problems began closing in on the housing scene.

Lot prices jumped madly as municipalities introduced ever more costly requirements and levies, and multiplied the delays before lots could be registered. Only expensive houses could absorb such high lot costs; and as ever more expensive houses came to be built, they proved beyond the means of most buyers. People found that they had to abandon their hope of owning a house, long considered a birthright of North Americans.

Instead, they had to resign themselves to renting an apartment. The high-rise apartment building became the mode of housing for a new generation of tenants. Some benefits came with this form: it appealed to the young, whose numbers were rapidly increasing because of our demographic curve; it suited non-family households that had become more common with changing life-styles. Fewer young unmarried people lived with their parents as had been the case in the past. Divorce, too, had become more common, and contributed to the demand for apartments. Immigrants arrived in mass without the means of acquiring a house. Apartments were convenient to older people whose families had left them.

Less apparent to the tenant was the growing opposition of ratepayers and municipal councils to this new type of housing. To the tenant, the municipal tax he paid was hidden as part of the rent he paid the landlord; accordingly assessments came to be rigged in favor of home-owners at the expense of apartment dwellers. In the City of Toronto in 1977 apartment buildings were assessed on the average at 26 percent of their market value as compared to 8.7 percent for individual houses.[1] Before long obstruction of further apartment lot zoning and levies had driven up the cost of apartment building lots per suite to the levels of house lot prices that had obtained only a few years earlier.

By 1975 the Canadian Government's price stabilization efforts had lifted first mortgage interest rates to 12 percent and even higher – compared to rates of six and six and one half percent in the later fifties. Since interest charges account for fully one half of gross rents, the effect on the industry was disastrous.

Still other factors were at work to put even apartment accommodation beyond the reach of many people. The immigrants who formed the core of the construction industry's labor force had become assimilated to Canadian living standards, which had also risen substantially since the war. Housing prices a generation ago had been made possible only because some of the workers in the building trades were receiving wages more than a little reminiscent of those of Calabria.

Early in the sixties the federal government unhinged the price structure of housing by imposing an 11 percent sales tax on building materials. This was followed by the Ontario government introducing a sales tax on the already taxed price of these materials that eventually rose to seven percent. At the time governments and their economic advisers failed to make the connection between such taxes and their inevitable effect in contributing to price essential housing out of the market.

In 1975, when high interest rates had finally sealed the fate of rental housing, the Ontario Government, along with other provinces, introduced rent controls. For instant political effect, the measure had much to commend it; but it led to the complete abandonment of the rental field by developers. Instead they turned to condominium apartments. These were thrown up in quantities that the market could not possibly absorb – not because they were not needed, but because they

1 Private communication from Mr. I. Nash of I. Nash Associates, assessment consultants.

were beyond the means of many who needed them.

'Affordability', a crucial concept in the economics of housing, is at best replete with uncertainty. It refers, to the ability of an individual to pay for housing. This depends upon the amount of his income, the portion of it available for housing, the security of that income into the distant future. It not only depends upon the general price level, but presupposes no unusual fluctuations in the prices of critical commodities and services such as fuel that determine the carrying costs of a house that is purchased. It also assumes that after a lifetime of sacrificing to pay for a home, that there will be a market for it on which the equity can be recovered when required. Today the impact of the post-war baby boom is contributing to the tightness of the housing market; in a decade, however, the problem may become one of too few buyers because of the falling birth rate of the latter 1960's.

How did we get into our present housing mess? Basically it was because those concerned with housing tried optimizing results by the logic of a single one of the many subsystems involved. They simply ignored the contraints imposed by the other subsystems. Inevitably, by a law enunciated by Forrester and quoted earlier in this book, the result was exactly contrary to what was expected.

Let me cite some instances of such one-system logic applied to housing.

Many of the urbanology studies that have appeared in recent years can only be described as exercises in landscape architecture and little else. They do not seek out the best compromise solution that would satisfy all the relevant subsystems: ecology, transportation, demography, unrenewable resources, construction costs, the price gradient, interest rates, and so forth. Instead, the emphasis is on the nostalgic attractions of low-density developments proper to small communities as they existed generations ago. On their own terms, there is nothing to be said against such essays, except that they ignore the problems of the population that could never be accommodated within such low-density zoning in our large cities.

A closely related instance of one-system reasoning is the formulation of housing standards in terms of categorical imperatives, with no reference to the means whereby the costs of such housing is to be met. And even if that were somehow contrived, there remains the further question of the opportunity costs to the very people whom such schemes are supposed to help – what other services needed by the same people would have to be forgone, because too great a portion of the resources available were spent on their housing.

Thus the insistence upon the right of low-income groups to new housing in the core of large cities because historically they have lived there becomes a tragic disillusionment when it is realised. The warehouses and factories that provide employment to unskilled and semiskilled workers have been migrating to the suburbs because of land costs, taxation and transport facilities. Even if it were economically feasible to resettle slum-dwellers in redeveloped downtown areas, it is by no means certain that we should be doing them a kindness.

By a strange quirk of British and North American tradition, the main burden of paying for municipal services and education has been put on real estate.[2] Partly because of this, many municipalities have resorted to every sort of delaying tactic to discourage the servicing of further lots; for servicing costs rise steeply per capita with increases in population. Within the logic of their subsystem, this might make good sense. Yet for housing the nation – and nations have become increasingly urbanized and thus dependent on such municipal decisions – it has been an unqualified disaster. With current high interest rates, delays of several years in the registration of lots can multiply their cost beyond recognition. Moreover, the high risks thus created must find reflection in correspondingly high profits expected by those who have faced such risks successfully. Otherwise no one would be prepared to take them.

When taxation makes housing unaffordable for a section of the population, its claim to shelter does not disappear. In our pluralistic society a minimum standard of housing is viewed as a right; when that becomes unaffordable on the market, the state is obliged to provide it

2 In *Housing Taxation and Housing Policy,* published in *The Economic Problems* of Housing (Proceedings of a Conference held by the International Economic Association). MacMillan, London, New York, 1967, edited by Adela Adam Nevitt, Richard Netzer gives real property taxes as percentages of Total Taxes and National Income:

	Percentage of	
	Total Tax Revenue	National Income
United States, 1962	12.6	3.5
Canada, 1961-2	15.8	5.1
United Kingdom, 1963	11.2	4.2
Austria, 1962	1.6	0.7
France, 1961-2	2.2	0.6
Germany, 1963	2.2	0.6
Norway, 1962	0.6	0.3

on a redistributional basis. When governments seek to solve their budgetary problems by loading more taxation on housing, foreseeable consequences ensue. A further portion of the private housing market is knocked out, and a corresponding burden is shifted onto the public sector. Invariably the cost of the state exceeds by far the amount of money that the taxes in question could possibly have brought in.

There is no ready solution for a problem as complex as that of housing in a modern urban community. But unless the whole problem is spelled out in terms of all the causal loops of the subsystems involved, we cannot know the alternatives that are really open to us.

We must, of course, begin with the constraints of the ecological system, not only as they exist today, but as they will exist in the years ahead. A house is a long-term investment and to assess its feasibility we cannot limit ourselves to present costs. Only by examining where the subsystems are leading can we avoid spurious short-cuts – e.g., inexpensive housing developments in areas that will require much travelling to places of employment, extravagantly low densities in large cities where the cost of services per foot frontage is certain to climb steeply.

Housing standards can be set only after such a study of available resources and costs. The most that can be said is that everybody has a right to the optimum *feasible* housing, but beyond that it is impossible to define housing needs in absolute terms. How many rooms? In what location? At what level of costs? With what amenities? With central air conditioning? Situated on how much land? Meaningful answers to such questions can only come from an examination of the relevant subsystems.

Ways must be found of enlisting the private sector for as much of the task of supplying society's housing as possible. Only when the means for doing this have been exhausted, should the state interevene with subsidies or public ownership.

It is self-defeating to put the brunt of the cost of urban services on residential housing, and on top of that, to add the burden of yet other taxes, open or hidden. For though this may be a convenience to the tax-collector, it undermines the ability of the private sector to perform in this crucial field. Before this situation can be remedied, we must somehow break out of the tight logics of the various levels of government. Each government, of course, has its own corporate metabolism. And yet in being guided by these, they are not contributing to the solution of the housing problem.

The role of our cities in our national life is vastly different from what it was a couple of generations ago. Somehow the fiscal responsibilities of the different levels of government must be reshuffled to reflect this. In our discussion I am assuming that this will be done, and I will refer in what follows to the pooled taxation of the three levels of government.

I will attempt to apply the technique of detaxation and taxbonding developed in this book to housing.

The streams of taxation enter housing costs by three distinct channels:

1) *The original cost of the housing including the builder's profit.*

This determines the mortgage amount which is usually set as a proportion of the selling price. The taxation that has entered the original cost is thus compounded by the mortgage interest, which often has been made needlessly high by mistaken stabilization policy. The cost of shelter is thus exposed to taxation and government error in a non-linear way.

2) *The carrying charges.*

Municipal taxes, we have seen, represent an inordinate part of the carrying charges of housing. Purely political considerations, too, have led to a disproportionate burden of the taxes levied on housing being placed on rental units through assessment bias. This has led to a distortion of zoning to provide not the housing that society needs and can afford, but housing that will bring in the maximum assessment. Taxes are usually collected on housing, whether it is occupied or not.

3) *Maintenance costs.*

These are driven up not only through taxes on materials, but by the high cost of shelter, which is an important determinant of tradesmen's wages. The high cost of shelter, we have see, reflects, in part, our present tax system.

When taxation through these three channels converges to put housing beyond the reach of a given income group, the government must step in to provide public housing for that group, or to subsidize private housing for that group. Each of these arrangements is uneconomical: not only in terms of absolute costs, but because of the effect on the negentropy of the private sector.

Nor can subsidies make good the damage caused by ill-considered taxation. The net effect of subsidizing and taxing the same industry is bound to be a negative one – not only because of the 'handling charges' in either direction, but for a more serious reason. The subsidy shifts fundamental decisions from the entrepreneur to the state. For in the last analysis it is the politicians who decide the terms on which the subsidy is granted. In this way a short-term political logic takes over and invades the various subsystems involved. Applying the modular congruence calculus explained in this book, a tax-cum-subsidy policy applied to the same industry appears as a harmful error.

PUBLIC HOUSING

When taxation makes it impossible for the private sector to provide shelter for a sector of the population, the state must step in with public housing. And the cost of that public housing will exceed the taxation that made it necessary. Such costs will not be limited to the operating deficits incurred. Hardly less important is the facts that the taxation needed to cover those deficits will add further to the price gradient, and will thus eat further into the affordability of housing. As a result still more public housing will be needed, and still more taxation.

Not even this covers the complete costs of public housing. In the private sector, investment is appraised not only by the original cost, but by the prospective return on such costs. Where there is no prospect of a return, the investment is written off as a loss. Such a criterion cannot be applied to public investment where it cannot be replaced with private investment. But where it can, a similar criterion must be applied to public investment if we are to make any meaningful comparisons.

Housing is a field where public and private investment are alternatives. We are always free to create conditions that will enable private entrepreneurs to provide the housing that the state is furnishing, if accounting shows that this is the more advantageous course. To fix comparable costs of public and private housing, we must therefore include a rapid write-off of the original cost as a non-productive (actually a losing) investment.

With society's tremendous capital needs in our day, this is hardly a minor point.

DETAXATION

Even from the standpoint of budgetary liquidity it is self-defeating to put the main burden of municipal services and local education on housing. In Toronto 25 percent of gross rents go to cover municipal taxes. This could be reduced to say, five percent in perhaps three stages. This would be achieved by equalizing the assessments of rental housing with those of owner-occupied housing, and by reducing the tax-rate on both.

Where sales taxes exists on building materials going into modest-priced housing, they should be removed. The range of the housing that should be detaxed is readily established — all housing receiving public subsidies in any form.

By leaching taxation out of the price of housing, we can to an extent reverse the scenario of the past few years. Through ill-considered taxation, governments have put the private sector out of business in certain critical areas only to find themselves burdened with the need of providing that housing themselves. When this happens, the cost of such housing is invariably far higher that what it was marketed for by the private sector.[3]

TAXBONDING

Clearly detaxation will leave a serious gap in state finances. But the price gradient that has arisen in our society presents a solution in this instance as well as a problem. The gradient brings about windfall profits in many industries; there is much to be said for the state appropiating part of these if that can be done without disturbing the negentropies of the private sector. The taxbond as a means of doing this has been explained earlier in this book. Entrepreneurs would be given the option of subscribing substantial portions of their taxable income in long-term bonds at low interest rates, rather than paying taxes on it. This would provide the state with a source of cheap money.

By applying this cheap money to mortgage financing, the interest rate on such loans could be reduced to perhaps six percent – less than half of what it was at the height of the latest stabilization effort of the Canadian Government. Such inexpensive money raised by taxbonds could also be made available to municipalities to help them lower their taxes. Combining the savings in mortgage interest and in taxation, it should be possible – in several stages – to reduce rents by as much as 40 percent.

Taxbonding and detaxing thus paired would be particularly rich in feedback effects.

Such a reduction of housing costs would extend affordability over wide ranges of the rental and purchase markets: people dependent upon the state in whole or in part for their shelter would be able to pay

3 *Ontario Ministry of Housing, Annual Report* 1975-6, p. 30, gives the operating loss on the rental units of the Ontario Housing Corporation, an official agency, at about $1,500 per unit. This omits the subsidy of the federal government hidden in the low interest rates of the mortgage on this housing. The loss, nevertheless, is over half the total rents of many private rental projects.

their own way. The public treasury would be relieved of a considerable burden. This would make possible a further reduction of taxation. That would temper the slope of the price gradient, and labor costs would tend to rise at a slower pace. This would make it possible to extend affordability to still further income brackets.

As the tax-base expanded with the reclaiming of more of the housing field by the private sector, a lower rate of taxation would bring in the same revenue. The effects of detaxation would thus snowball.

As more of the housing industry reverted to the private sector, the state could devote itself to the general guidance in the field. Released from constant short-term crises, it could devote its resources to doing those things that the private sector alone cannot do: providing the infrastructures, producing the necessary trunk services, and programming for the long-term constraints imposed by our resources and ecological systems. The collaboration of the public and private sectors would be put on a new, sounder basis.

CAUSAL LOOP MODEL OF 'VANISHING SHELTER'.

In this model a number of related events occur simultaneously as they evolve through time. Decisions by the municipality influences the builder in making his construction plans. The arrival upon the market of large numbers of young people who have reached the age where they consider renting or buying shelter add to the extent of the problem. These and other factors interact to create the complex nature of our housing system. Complex systems result from feedback loops that often cause the system to be intractable to change by simplistic policy. However, properly studied, complex systems may offer points where pressures can be applied to alter or restore the system balance.

This paper submits that such a point of influence pressure in the housing system is fiscal, involving taxation and interest rates. The present policies were accumulated in the course of time as governments imposed taxation where they found it most expedient. Measures of this sort reinforced each other, and their unforeseen effect was to stop construction of all but expensive houses that are beyond the reach of most buyers. The model diagram attempts to show the ramification of these fiscal effects as they operate at present, and what the consequence of their removal might be.

The diagram of cause and effect relationships, which we call a 'causal loop diagram', depicts the stalemate in the construction of affordable housing. Because of the developing price gradients in the systems,

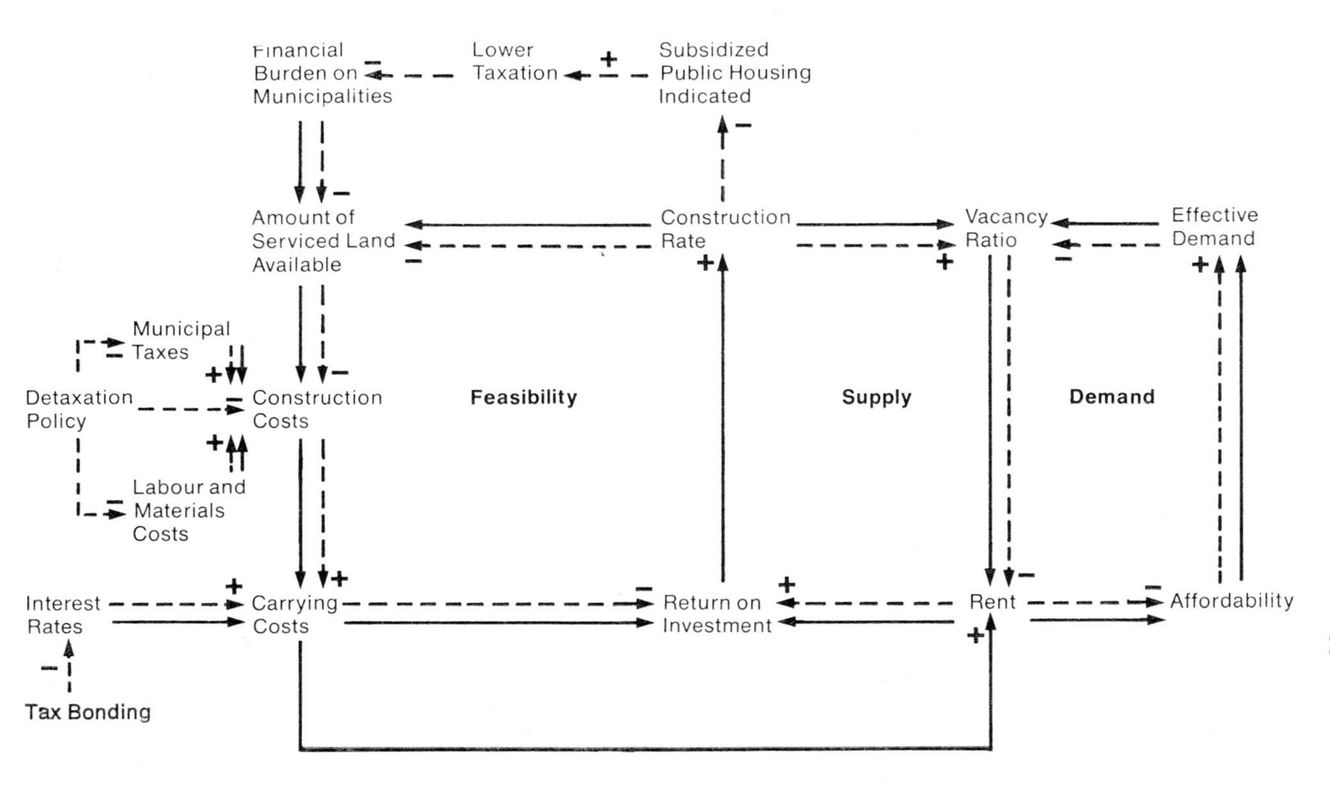

Financial Burden on Municipalities
Lower Taxation
Subsidized Public Housing Indicated
Amount of Serviced Land Available
Construction Rate
Vacancy Ratio
Effective Demand
Municipal Taxes
Detaxation Policy
Construction Costs
Feasibility
Supply
Demand
Labour and Materials Costs
Interest Rates
Carrying Costs
Return on Investment
Rent
Affordability
Tax Bonding

there is also implication that if present trends continue, people who have their homes or apartments may not be able to meet their rents, or carrying costs.

The loops of the diagram show the factors that determine the feasibility of construction, the supply and demand of housing, the return on investment, and the circumstances that make for subsidies and public housing. The model is also used to simulate reversal of present trends by policies of detaxation and taxbonding.

The feasibility of construction.

In judging whether a construction project is feasible, the builder must weigh costs against likely returns. The cost components are shown as inputs to the feasibility loops. The *financial burden on municipalities* prompts them to add to the cost of *serviced land* and impose high municipal taxes. The discouragement of further residential construction within their borders complies with the wishes of their constituency. These factors, along with the costs of *labor* and *materials,* contribute to *construction costs.* The *interest rates* on the loans to finance these construction costs generate a major part of the carrying costs which the investor must meet. Such carrying costs set the floor under the expected *rent,* or, in the case of purchase housing, limit the affordability for buyers.

By comparing the carrying costs with the likely rents – determined in part by the relationship of supply and demand – the builder can estimate the eventual return in his investment. The *construction rate* that results from this comparison adds housing units to the market, and consumes the supply of serviced land.

Supply and Demand.

As new housing units come onto the market, they add to the *vacancy ratio* if they are not sold or rented at once. A high vacancy ratio will tend to depress price. The high carrying costs and the general price gradient, however, act as a buffer against any significant lowering of price. Due to this price remains pegged at a level above what the market can afford.

Eventually the vacancy ratio is determined by *effective demand,* as expressed by the number of renters who can afford to pay the rents asked, or the buyers who can meet both the down payments and the monthly carrying obligations incurred. Today the number of renters and buyers who satisfy this *affordability* criterion is a decreasing proportion of the total number of potential buyers. The problem intensified by the entry outo the housing market of the bumper crop of post-war babies who have now reached full adulthood.

The basic cause of the present housing stalemate is the absence of affordable units. As the causal diagram shows, there is no likelihood that this condition will right itself in response to spontaneous forces, because it was not caused by such factors.

With the scarcity of affordable housing, the authorities are under pressure to build *public housing* and to grant *subsidies* to both builders and tenants. A condition that was to a large extent caused by high taxes and policy-induced interest rates has come full circle. It has led to the disbursement of more public money in subsidies and public housing than was collected in the form of the taxation that caused the market dislocations. In addition, new government bureaucracies have had to be set up to administer the state contributions. This adds yet another layer of cost. presumably paid for by more *taxation,* and adding further to the *financial burden of the* municipalities.

Detaxation and Taxbonding

The broken lines in the causal diagram show the effects of *detaxation* and *taxbonding* proposed in the paper. The removal of fiscal constraints that inhibit the system will lower *carrying costs and rents.* This will make housing affordable to a group of buyers and renters whose numbers increase in greater proportion than the drop in rent and costs.[4]

This will restore employment in the construction industry as it makes available housing to middle and lower-income buyers. The public authorities are relieved of the need for subsidies and unemployment insurance payments.

4 The 1971 Census of Canada (Statistics Canada, Part 1, Bulletin 3, 1-1, November, 1976) gives the declared revenue of population of 15 years and over in the following distribution:

$ 5,000 to	$ 5,999	895,285	individuals
6,000 "	6,999	831,290	"
7,000 "	7,999	737,770	"
8,000 "	8,999	588,390	"
9,000 "	9,999	418,565	"
10,000 "	11,999	540,845	"
12,000 "	14,999	354,155	"
15,000 "	19,999	210,420	"

If we adjust by a factor 1.7 to allow for price movement between 1971 and 1977, and add one third for average additional earnings by other members of the family, we have the following crude approximation of the distribution of family income. If we take 25 percent of family income as the maximum to determine affordability in the case of rental housing we arrive at the following populations for the different affordability brackets:

25 percent of family income (arithmetic mean of bracket)	Number of families in bracket (assuming 1.33 earners per family)
$9,890	157,890
7,631	265,616
6,275	405,653
5,373	313,923
4,804	441,293
4,239	553,328
3,673	623,469
3,109	671,164

If we bring rents down from $3,673 per annum to $3,109, or 15.3%, we increase the number of families who can afford apartments from 2,761,121 (the total population of the higher brackets) to include a further 671,464 families. At that point of the affordability-rent level curve, for every percent decrease in rents, affordability goes up 1.6 percent.

INDEX

OTHER BOOKS BY WILLIAM KREHM

PRICE IN A MIXED ECONOMY: OUR RECORD OF DISASTER

The basic work in which the theory of pluralistic price is developed in depth. It is indispensable for an understanding of our economy today.
Cloth $13.95 Paperback $9.95

* * * * * *

For Autumn Publication 1978

HOW TO MAKE MONEY IN A MISMANAGED ECONOMY

The author establishes that our policy-makers are steering by a misleading economy theory, and as a result are without a clue as to the real effects of their policies. Taking this fact as a datum, he explores its consequences for the investor. From the concepts of structural price gradient, entropy, and system dynamics developed in his earlier works, he deduces some fundamental business strategies for these troubled times.

This book is essential for the intelligent businessman, civil servant and economist. It draws heavily upon the author's lengthy experience in applying his theories with success in the business world.
Cloth $13.95 Paperback $8.95

THORNWOOD PUBLICATIONS
141 Avenue Road,
Toronto, Ontario M5R 2H7, Canada